I0138886

THE POWER OF HIS BRUSH

The Evolution Of R.C. Gorman

Nikos Ligidakis

INKWELL™ BOOKS

Writing - Publishing - Printing

THE POWER OF HIS BRUSH
The Evolution Of R.C. Gorman

Copyright © 2017 by Nikos Ligidakis

All Rights Reserved.
No part of this book may be reproduced, stored in a retrieval system,
or transmitted by any means, electronic, mechanical, photocopying,
recording, or otherwise, without written permission from the publisher.

This book is based on a true story. To protect the privacy of
individuals, some names have been changed, some characteristics
have been revised and some dialogue has been recreated. All thoughts
reflect the author's research recollections of experiences over time. All
contents in this book are the responsibility and faults of the author.

ISBN 978-1-939625-83-0
Library of Congress Control Number: 2017905365

Published by Inkwell Books LLC
10632 North Scottsdale Road, Unit 695
Scottsdale, AZ 85254
Tel. 480-315-3781

E-mail info@inkwellbooksllc.com
Website www.inkwellbooksllc.com

PROLOGUE

During my visits to the R.C. Gorman Navajo Galleries, I watch people's reactions to looking at Gorman's art and interviewing them; I gain a deeper understanding of his art.

The artistic process, especially with complicated minds like Gorman's, stimulates unusually thoughtful reflection. It is challenging to look at images and infer the ideas they represent. What pushes our understanding is the continual stream of good questions; questions are the catalyst that steered me to a more profound meaning about what guided the artist to design the images he constructed. *"The aim of art is to represent not the outward appearance of things, but their inward significance,"* Aristotle wrote.

Undoubtedly, R.C. Gorman's art helped many people process their emotions and understand their surroundings, allowed them to see life from a different perspective, and made them feel alive. I understood that as beautiful as art may be, its resolve goes beyond beautifying the walls of a space.

Art holds the power to open your heart, nourish your mind, and channel your inner awareness, bringing us closer to our truest selves.

Because of the deeper understanding of R.C. Gorman's art, writing The Power of His Brush, The Evolution of RC Gorman, was a labor of love.

1

HIS MOUNTAINS

Beneath the winding road, the currents of the Rio Grande River moved slowly through the large cottonwood-dominated forest canyon. In the distance, beyond the treetops, a mystic gloominess blanketed across the mountains, creating a captivating beauty.

As I drove further up and approached the eight-thousand foot altitude, majestic mountains dominated the roadside and threatening dark clouds hung over my head. A few miles before the top, the first airy snowflakes glazed the red rocks and limited my visibility. As I made my way from the stunning southwest landscape into the flat open-faced Native American land, the snowflakes increased in size and number and eventually turned the town of Taos into a pure white spectacle.

Taos, New Mexico is well known for its artistic society. It is a city chock-full of art galleries, some of which are located around the charming Ledoux Street.

The purpose of my trip to Taos was to deepen my knowledge of one of the most fascinating and legendary artists to grace this mountaintop town, a man that I had never met. My challenge was that I had to chase his ghost since this man physically left this earth over ten years ago.

As I walked up to his studio gallery, I pause for a moment trying to understand why so many artists have chosen this place to live and create their art. Even though the snowflakes kept falling, the sky was visibly blue, and I felt the overwhelming presence of the mountains that tower around this area.

The building which was standing in front of me served as R.C. Gorman's home, studio and gallery. It was here that he created and exhibited his unique art.

I felt a sense of nostalgia as I entered the place where he spent the better part of his life. Maybe it was the wooden floors, the old southwestern element or the spirit of Gorman himself that was notable in every nook of this place. My mind went back to a time of classical romanticism, a time when art consumed the social makeup and artists passionately devoted their entire existence to doing what they loved most.

Against the large front glass window, his brushes, palettes, and small Navajo pottery adorned a long table made of raw wood and dotted with drops of paint. This was where he liked to work; under the sunlight and overlooking the mountain tops. Deeper into the room sat an antique desk with an arm-chair in front of it. Oil paintings from the earlier days, as well as masks, pottery, Navajo rugs, large textiles, and the contemporary art that made him famous were displayed on the walls and various tables around the room. The display showed the astounding journey of Gorman's rebellious artistic mind, a story of progression from the early days until the end. He left an impressive milestone.

A fireplace and an antique desk with a sign "Virginia Dooley" on top of it decorated the room, next to it there was the kitchen where Gorman, and his friends spent endless hours practicing his other passion; cooking.

Wooden steps led to a bedroom on the upstairs floor.

I sat on a chair in the front of the gallery before leaving, to spend a few more moments in this complacent element. In my mind's eye appeared the times when common folk and celebrities alike flocked to this place to meet Gorman and to have a moment with his charming presence.

Recently there was an opening of a new gallery on Paseo De Pueblo Norte Street, just a short distance from R.C. Gorman's studio. Even though the weather seemed a bit harsh to me, people flocked there. Taos is an artist's town after all. The new gallery was a large mud mansion in the Taos Historic District. Featured art included legendary classic Native American artists and exhibits of newer contemporary work of American Indigenous artists.

I was there to meet Gregorio for the first time, the young man whose lifelong dream was to open a gallery to honor Native American art. In the center of the room, there was a life-size bronze statue of R.C. Gorman with a beautiful Navajo mantra wrapped around his shoulders to keep him warm. Gregorio did not have to introduce himself; I knew exactly who he was. He stood proud next to Gorman's statue wearing a bright turquoise suit, a light blue shirt and a deep blue western bolo tie. He had a thick beard and his hair was tied back into a bun. His face opened up to a great welcoming smile when I told him who I was. We had spoken several times over the phone in the past few months.

"Welcome," he said.

"This is charming," I replied.

After a bit of small talk, I asked him about Gorman. He had never met Gorman but worked in his studio gallery for several years.

"R.C. Gorman is my art hero," he began. "When I lived in his studio I felt him all around me. I remember one time I was taking a bath in his small bathtub; I lit some candles and I played classical music just like he used to do. I closed my eyes, and I imagined his hand moving with the sound of the music, just like a conductor, leaving behind lines of vivid colors. People who watch him paint always said that it was like looking at a conductor at a symphony."

He continued to talk for a while about Gorman; his words emotional, and his admiration for the artist was evident.

"I designed my gallery to feature legendary artists along side new and upcoming ones. If R.C. was here, it would be the way he wanted it to be. Sometimes he would refuse to do a showing unless a new artist was featured along with him."

I strolled around his gallery; in addition to Gorman's, there were works of notables and some unknown artists as well as North American petroglyph art, jewelry, pottery, carvings, and textile.

"Make no mistake; Gorman was well-read, just like most of the giants of the art. He regularly read history, philosophy, religion and anything he could get his hands on."

We decided to meet again; there was so much to talk about.

As I walked outside, something that he said earlier was stuck in my brain, "R.C. Gorman stayed in Taos because the mountains spoke to him! He felt a strong connection with the mountains."

Early the next morning, I came down from my room in the old elegant southwest style historic hotel located in the center of the town plaza. As I entered the coffee shop by the lobby, I reflected on the anomaly between the classical southeastern charms blended with a modern luxury coffee shop. As I sat in a table next to an old-bearded mountain-looking man talking to a young couple holding iPhones, the anomaly all around me seemed absorbing.

I usually do not eavesdrop, but the old mountain-man was talking about the town, its history and, what I found most interesting, the mountains surrounding the town.

"Personally, I have not experienced it, but for the longest time, many people talked about low-frequency humming sounds in Taos Pueblo. People who could hear it describe feeling blessed and comforted by the low-frequency noise."

Doing some research, I discover that the place he was most likely talking about was the peak of El Salto. For generations, the people of the area have considered El Salto to be a holy mountain.

Taos is nestled deep within the Sangre de Cristo mountain range as is the old Taos Pueblo, home of the Tiwa Indians, one of the longest inhabited communities and a highly cultural and spiritual town. Legend has it that one of the mystical dimensions of Taos Pueblo is the "Taos Hum."

The majestic peak of El Salto has several waterfalls that descend its slopes. Behind the waterfalls, along with the various elevations of the mountain, are caves of different shapes. Under the setting sun, the peaks reflects the reddish colors which caused the first settlers in the valley to name the entire range Sangre de Cristo, or "Blood of Christ".

I headed up the mountains with high hopes that I would be able to hear the humming, although I was confident that the mountains could not talk. They are made of stones and dirt after all but, as always, I kept an open mind.

From the parking area at the end of El Salto Road, it is less than a half a mile to reach the first waterfall. The trail followed the bottom of a rocky cliff and emerged at the waterfall. The water spilled forcefully over the top of a dramatic cave into a pool below. The other waterfalls are above this one and reaching them requires climbing a steep trail and rock ledges. It is the caves in the back of the waterfalls that cause the sound of the water to echo throughout the valley. On different levels of the mountain, people hear low or high 'hums' as reported with many mountain climbers who have taken the time to climb upward. The old man spoke about a humming coming from the mountains. I could not hear it, but I was not connected to the mountains like many of those living around them. Then again, I am a man from the blue sea. My skin is soaked by the salty blue water of the Aegean and dried by the warm sun of the Mediterranean sky. I am not a mountain-man and snow falling is a foreign element to me. However, on this trip to the mountain town and the visit to mountaintops, I grew to appreciate the mesmerizing beauty of this land and in a fashion I heard it – the mountains "spoke" to me in a way that I had no choice but to listen.

As I drove down the mountain I felt I had the knowledge of how they spoke to Gorman and why this place was an inspiring source for him.

Now, my challenge was to comprehend what it was about this man named R.C. Gorman, for whom celebrities made the trip to Taos just to meet him; for whom people were in awe speaking about him. He was a man who needed no name introduction because he was simply recognized by his radiant smile, the colorful bandannas, and his florid Hawaiian shirts.

My quest to find R.C. Gorman has just begun.

THE POWER OF HIS BRUSH
The Evolution Of R.C. Gorman

2

DEEP ROOTS

In the early 1900's it was unusual to hear, in a remote Navajo reservation, extraordinary voices of beauty and grace by grand opera singers. Singers like the great Enrico Caruso, Geraldine Farrar, Amelita Galli-Curci, and many others. Their voices soared out of the wide horn of the old gramophone and dispersed into the narrow streets of the neighborhoods. The rhythmical classical music from *La Traviata, Rigoletto, I Pagliacci,* accompanied by the high vocal range of the tenors was an unexpected sound for those who walked outside the long adobe home. This peculiar music was part of this remote community in warm summer evenings and wind whistled, snow falling winter nights. Eventually its continual play began to breed familiarity and enjoyment to other people around.

Inside this home, by the mouth of Canyon de Chelly in the small community of Chinle, Arizona, a mother, a thin Navajo woman was weaving at her small loom. Her hands, lifting the harnesses, moved to the sound of the music. Her feet followed, stepping on the treadles, moving from left to right, and right to left. The body rocking side-to-side as the legs pedaled the treadles, then leaning forward and gliding back as the beater of the loom hammers the yarn, pushing it solidly in place. The music ascents, the tenor's voice soars upwards, the sound and movement are now rhythmical; left-right-and-back.

From shuttle to the beater, time and again the hands direct the rhythmic sounds of the music, the voice and the loom. Her body leads this dance by the drumming of her loom – a mesmerizing symphony of sounds.

A mother glanced periodically at her older daughter, Mary, who was reading to her little brother Wallace with the help of a kerosene lamp. Her second child, Carl, was sitting on the floor drawing on paper and baby Stephen was encased in his cradleboard. Carl often sat next to his mother to watch, intrigued by her weaving. He would follow the tapestry of color and the design created before his eyes, just like a beautiful painting.

It was time for mother Alice to prepare dinner for the family since father Nelson Gorman was to be home after a long day's work. She threw some wood into the pot-belly stove standing in the middle of the living room before walking into her kitchen; it was going to be a cold night. The music would play during and after dinner. The children listened, Mary liked to read and Carl loved drawing with his pencil.

The father, Nelson Gorman, was a tall, thin, hard-working man with ambition to become a successful businessman. He operated a highly prosperous trading post that was attached in front of their house and later opened another one on Black Mountain. He also owned a ranch with many horses and over a thousand cattle that roamed in the long ridge from Chinle to the Black Mountain. It was at that ranch that his son, Carl fell in love with horses.

It was because of his father's hard work and good business sense as well his mother's ingenuity that Carl witnessed several new things in the reservation. For instance, the old Model T Ford his father brought home which was used for family outings. His mother, determined to build a refrigerator, created a large wooden box outside the kitchen window, covered it with layers of thick burlap and, from a small water tank above the box, water dripped down steadily into the box. The dripping water evaporated taking away the heat from the inside and leaving the wooden chamber cool.

Alice was an accomplished weaver who also worked with Presbyterian missionaries. She loved nature and horses. She was born near the towering peaks of the Chuska Mountains, in the Navajo Land of New Mexico. It was a land full of green valleys studded with ponderosa and oak trees which spread across the rolling hills. There were herds of cattle, sheep and horses running free. Alice made sure that her children knew the history of their people. Her children learned that their paternal great-grandfather was part of the historic long walk back to their homeland after four years of the Navajo imprisonment. While in prison, he learned the art of silver-smithing, which, he taught to the rest of his tribe upon his return to the motherland.

The ancient home of the Anasazi originated in the Canyon de Chelly National Monument in northeastern Arizona. This canyon is not as spectacular as other Arizona canyons, but it is a mystical place that provides a fascinating insight into the life of the Navajo. From the Anasazi civilization of the twelfth century to the Navajo tribe who lived here for over three hundred years, this area served its inhabitants as a refuge from their enemies.

Shortly after you enter the Canyon, the rocky walls rise sharply making this the only possible entrance and a fortress where the Navajo felt protected from their Spanish and Anglo enemies. The canyon land, adorned with the scattered ancient ruins, remains fertile and green most of the year. The astounding combination of the rocky walls, the beauty of the landscape and safety are the reasons why the valley has been inhabited for so long.

Traditionally the Navajos are nomadic in spirit and, since their emergence into an identifiable culture in the seventeenth century, they often moved to areas near their fields for hunting and trading and where they could seek the mountains for their inspiration. Eventually, they settled in the corners of northeastern Arizona, northwestern New Mexico and southeastern Utah, to be near the most dependable sources of water, fertile land, hunting grounds and most importantly, a short distance from the mountains, which are sacred for the Navajos. They claimed this empty land as their own and built the Navajo nation.

The Navajo people chose to live far from the colonists after learning a lesson from the Pueblo's destruction by the Spanish.

The Pueblo Revolt of the1680's was a result of Spain's definition of colonization by conquering the lands of the Pueblo people and imposing imperialism and Catholicism. Because of the drought that swept the region ten years before the revolt, the Pueblos, hungry and poor were forced into slavery.

Forward almost two-hundred years later, the devastation of the Navajos did not come from a foreign enemy but from people who were guests in their land. The United States, after their victorious war with Mexico in 1848, claimed that Navajo land was a United States property. The Navajos were caught by surprise and pledged to protect their land. The dominant United States Army, led by Colonel Kit Carson, arrived in force and devastated the Navajo homeland. The surviving Navajos, demoralized and starving were deported from their land and forced to march over three-hundred-seventy miles to the Bosque Redondo concentration camp on the Pecos River. During the long walk, hundreds, and later in the camp, thousands of Navajos died from hunger, exhaustion and smallpox.

The Navajo Treaty of 1868, signed with the United States, freed over eight thousand Navajos after four years of imprisonment and returned them to their homeland, now reduced to a much smaller size. They began rebuilding their lives and their herds, virtually unnoticed in an area that most Americans considered worthless desert wasteland.

Carl, now ten years old, along with his younger brother Wallace, following their mother's wishes to learn the Christian faith, were separated from their culture to attend the Rehoboth Mission School. This was a boarding school started by Christian missionaries who came to the Southwest in the late 1800's to bring the Gospel to the Navajo and Zuni people. The school was built in the Gallup, New Mexico area, prohibited children to speak their native language. They were forced to only speak English. Carl and his brother were punished repeatedly for refusing to speak English exclusively.

The school had a reputation of the rigid belief, "Accept our faith or

10

else!" The punishment for those who disobeyed was to be beaten up or locked in a room for an extended period with very little food.

At the first opportunity, the boys ran away and returned to their family.

It turned out that this revolutionary act brought Carl to the crossroads that would determine his identity.

Young Carl began to develop a healthy relationship with his father while they worked together on the ranch and while riding with him on long treks. They would drive cattle northeast to Round Rock or south to Ganado Ridge and back, over thirty miles each way. They rode in the heart of America, through the swirling red-earth desert winds that rattled their horses and cattle, through jagged rocks, sandstone pinnacles, buttes, and flat orange mesas. The panoramic views, amazing and unforgettable, remained intact in Carl's young mind. Sheep and goats grazed on the slopes of their sacred mountains, they passed wild mustangs and burros roaming around sagebrush, pinon pines and in narrow canyons.

When the last bright colors of the setting sun shimmered on the parched horizon, father and son prepared to camp for the night.

Navajos central belief is living in harmony with the earth and that everything is alive, interconnected and sacred. The Navajo people preferred to sleep on the compacted red earth of a wood and mud Hogan, designed with four pillars facing the cardinal points, a spiral ceiling pointing to the sky and a door facing east to welcome the rising sun. They are taught to respect the divine, their heritage and the knowledge of their healers. The Medicine Man, usually a sharp weathered face brightened by elaborate turquoise jewels around his neck, awakens a strong power coming from the earth and sees your life reflected in the fire on the floor. He fans your body with eagle feathers while chanting and palming sweet cedar smoke across your face to bless and purify you.

"In our beliefs, there are many different Gods; The wind, the rain, and the sunlight. We live close to these holy spirits so when we make a ceremony like this they come to witness." the Medicine Man would tell you.

The rising of the sunlight reflected on red rock walls around the camping grounds where Carl and his father spent a night of rest on their long trek driving cattle. There were no tall buildings or people wandering on busy streets when he opened his eyes, just the breathtaking beauty of the land, rolling hills, wild horses, and sunlight illuminating the earth.

It was a time that young Carl bonded with the beauty of the countryside, the richness of the mountains and the pride of the Navajo.

His mother always insisted that he speak English at home but, during the long rides with his father they spoke in Navajo. The knowledge of the world outside the reservation, the heartfelt classical music, the pride of his heritage, the beauty of the land and his love for horses, became an explosive compound inside of him. It was the birthing of the principal foundation of his philosophy of how to overcome life's hardships and an important component of his artistic mind. Carl Gorman had seen two worlds – both equally important. The primary one was the world of his people, but there was another world that slipped through the cracks of harmony and balance with the earth and spirit. He realized that his world stood between the fabric of the surrounding, the other, the modern world, a world that he had to accept and coexist

.

3

THE FIRST STEPS

On a hot day in July of 1931, Rudolph Carl Gorman came to this world surrounded by people with deep convictions of culture, family and tradition. His people thrived on positive energy that generated from the earth, the sun, the stars, lightning, fire and the gleaming colors of the rainbow. Growing up, to the people on the reservation, he was Rudy. Later in life his friends called him R.C. but the world would get to know him as R.C. Gorman.

Rudy was born in the midst of the economic depression.

Unemployment was high, the value of livestock fell dramatically, demand for sheep's wool was nonexistent and thus, income from his father's ranch dropped considerably.

He was the offspring of Carl Gorman and Adele Katherine Brown, married over a year before his birth. Adele, a beautiful woman, had just returned to the reservation to work for the Bureau of Indian Affairs after graduating with a Home Economics degree from the Indian school in Riverside, California. It was there that Carl fell madly in love with her. Carl and Adele had two more children Donna and Donald.

Rudy's mother, to direct him towards the Anglo world, spoke to him only in English and pushed him towards the white man's beliefs. She insisted on being a Catholic and sent him to attend the Catholic Boarding

School on the Navajo reservation. The model of boarding schools was adopted a few decades before Rudy was forced to join one. Native American children were separated from their families and taken to boarding schools far from their reservations. The majority of these schools were sponsored by religious denominations.

When children arrived in these schools, their lives were altered dramatically. Traditionally, many tribes were told to wear long hair with pride to honor their ancestors, yet, in the boarding schools, they were given short haircuts. They were given uniforms, English names and were not allowed to speak their languages at any time. They were also forced to convert to Christianity. Discipline was stiff in many schools and it often included severe punishments. Many of these schools were run by military personnel and the daily routines were based on military principals.

From the moment Rudy arrived at the boarding school, he realized that he was there to be taught how not to be "an Indian". He rebelled and refused the idea of not being a Navajo. He was not about to forget his tribal beliefs, no matter what the punishment was. He yearned to be back with his people; to be around the celebrations, the dances, the songs, the foods. He liked his hair long and proudly wore his "savage" clothes.

This was a time Native American-controlled school systems became non-existent while the Native Americans were made captives of federal or mission education to help students learn about the dominant European history and to convert to Christianity.

Eventually, over fifty million acres of land was taken away from Native American control.

After rebellious opposition of not following the rules of the Catholic Boarding School, he was expelled.

He then entered the Ganado Presbyterian Mission School. There he was allowed to speak his language and was allowed to upheld the traditional Navajo religious practices. His teachers encouraged his art and played a significant role in his inspiration to become a full-time artist. However, his primary influence to remain focused on his art was Rudy's grandmother. She spent quality time with him during his childhood; they herded sheep together, sang the old songs, she taught him to respect plants and animals and encouraged him to draw images on rocks. His grandmother helped raise him, recounting Navajo legends and enumerating his genealogy of artist ancestors. She kindled his desire to become an artist and told him to never forget the Navajo traditions and legends.

When a Grandmother speaks in a Navajo family, everyone stops and listens. Rudy was also very attached to his father who was his childhood hero. They reared sheep and goats in the canyon, planted crops, and, later on when his father became an accomplished painter, R.C. was his father's biggest fan.

When the Navajo were called for duty, after President Roosevelt declared war against Japan on December 8, 1941, Carl Gorman was one of the original twenty-nine Navajos who developed the Navajo code to be used in communication during the war, a code that the Japanese were never able to break. The Code Talker's use of the Navajo language for radio communication in the field proved so effective that recruitment for the program was expanded. Eventually, over four-hundred Navajo Code Talkers saw duty in the Pacific. Carl Gorman was a proud US marine.

As a child, Carl had been punished for speaking Navajo, but during the war, he would use his native language to save American lives in the Pacific.

After World War II, most Native American Code Talkers returned to communities that were having difficult economic times. Jobs were scarce and so were opportunities for education or job training. Racism toward the Native American people was common and even though they had served their country with distinction, Native American veterans could not eat or drink in some establishments - or even vote in some national or state elections.

War was hard on the entire American economy. Food and gasoline were rationed and many basic items were in short supply. After the war, many returning veterans found it difficult to find jobs. Most American Indian reservations and communities are located in rural areas where there are few jobs even during normal economic times. Unemployment and poverty levels had long been high for Native Americans, but it was even worse after the war

Rudy watched his Dad as he embraced success, hardship, and survived personal tragedy. He demonstrated the resilience of spirit that has been inspirational to all who knew him.

R.C. Gorman was with his Dad when he was at his best and at his worst. His dad lived through an unimaginable tragedy, one that almost put an end to his successful career as an artist.

Art remained a big part of Navajo life. In the early twentieth century, many Navajo painters created art that combined traditional with nontraditional style and form. Noted for their precise detail, restrained palette, and elegance of line, in both watercolors and oil paintings, they flourished and became famous beyond their communities.

4

THE POWER OF HIS BRUSH

What defines the city of Santa Fe is the amazing sunsets, the earthy adobe architecture, the endless art galleries, historic museums and, most important, the celebration of cultures. A combination of Native American, Hispanic, and Anglo influence is the core of this unique city. The blend of cultures and art creates a distinct spirit which is unmistakably Santa Fe.

The natural beauty of the landscape and the quality of light in the high desert was the primary appeal that drew artists to Santa Fe in the early twentieth century. Orientation to the natural environment is fundamental to the artist and this natural element is profound in both cities of Santa Fe and Taos. In Gorman's studio in Taos, there was an animating influence of light. The way sunlight moved through space, along with the integrating shadowiness of the surrounding mountains created certain forms, colors and substance, inspiring his artistic imagination. It was in his studio in Taos that Gorman created most of his masterpieces.

On my way back to Arizona, the rainy weather of Taos was replaced with the delicate blue sky adorned with a plethora of white clouds. By the time I stopped in Santa Fe to visit Gorman's art gallery, the clouds had turned to gray. I walked by the historic Santa Fe Plaza, in the center gathering place in town, surrounded by the beat of music from street musicians playing on the sidewalks. The energy was lively and positive.

People walked around slowly, children chasing pigeons, tourists buying wares from vendors. There were unique boutiques, small eateries, souvenir shops, old bookshops, art galleries, and local native artists selling their jewelry and artwork. On the green area in the center of the plaza, there were food vendors and people walking their dogs.

A gentle breeze tickled my nose with a cocktail of grilled meats and freshly brewed coffee. The drops of a misty rain begin to splatter onto the sidewalk. An elderly street performer kept playing his violin, enduring the raindrops. I stopped for a moment to admire his trueness; he did not even glance at me – lost in his music. I quickened my pace while the clouds began to gather in the sky. By the time I arrived at the gallery, the sky darkened and the rainfall intensified. In a few steps, I moved from an obscure gloomy, wet world into a celebrated world of vibrant colors projected from the walls of the large showroom and restrained only by curved lines so precisely arranged that only a masterful hand could have done it. The large showroom was carefully planned to allow visitors to view the exhibited art at the comfort of their own pace. The people, despite the rain, were faithfully walking the room. It took a few moments to begin to register the colorful setup as my eyes adjusted to the brightness of the art and a few more extra moments to grasp the beauty that surrounded me. I noticed some people prolonged their steps to marvel the art, realizing that they had now entered into the serenity and positive light that is the artwork of a true legend.

When I first visited Gorman's gallery in Scottsdale, Arizona some time ago I knew very little about his art. It took me a few visits to grasp the genius of his work. For me, it was a slow growth into the simplistic web of his lines and colors. The more I examined his art, the more my fascination grew along with my curiosity.

In my last stop before I left Taos, I visited Gorman's art Gallery there. In the much smaller showroom, I watched in amazement as a middle-aged woman stood in front of a Gorman painting shedding tears. I had never witness such a scene in front of works of visual art. I have seen people have strong emotional reactions while listening to music or watching a movie and have done so myself.

My curiosity was so overwhelming that I dared to disrespect her intimate space and quietly stood a few feet next to her. Eventually she looked at me; she did not attempt to hide her tears. She smiled a fainted smile really.

"Do you like this painting?" I asked.

She quickly glanced at it. "It's my favorite."

I heard the crack in her voice. It was obvious by the way she looked at the painting, it intrigued a defining memory.

The name of the painting was *Jubilee*. A young Native American woman is dressed in the typical Gorman distinctive red-colored top, extending her arms to let a white dove fly towards the sky.

"What is it about this one that moves you so deeply?"

"Today is my wedding anniversary." Her voice draws back. She takes a breath and raises her shoulders slightly. "I just love the meaning of this painting."

I remained silent, sensing that she was about to explain the meaning.

"My husband loved R.C.'s work. Our first trip was, in Taos to see his studio and visit his graveside. Since my husband passed away three years ago, I make frequent trips to Taos to reminisce. It brings me closer to my husband."

I looked at the painting. Now I could see what she was seeing; a young woman letting go of the symbol for peace and tranquility and directing it to the heavens. "I am trying to deal with my struggle, to let him go but I cannot yet." She paused.

I stood speechless from a sheer sense of mixed emotions. She introduced the painting to me the way I had never seen before.

"Thank you for putting it in perspective." I said looking at the dove aiming for the sky. She smiled and walked away. "Good luck..." I whispered.

On my way to Santa Fe, I thought about the lady's tears and the girl's hands letting the dove fly. A mixture of sadness and joy swirled in my heart for someone whose name I did not even know.

Here, in the Santa Fe's showroom, the mood was different.

I walked around to see people's reaction and to solicit information from visitors about their knowledge and feelings. An older couple was sitting on a leather bench. She was holding his hand tightly as if she did not want to let him go. His face was sad and she had a faded smile on her lips. They were staring at a painting called *Dream Night*. It is a woman floating towards the star-studded sky, hands crossed over her heart, her head lifted with her eyes yearning for higher layers of the heavens.

A young woman was meditating in front of *Navajo Mother in Supplication*. It shows a mother kneeling, her entire body curved around her baby laying on a blanket, her arms cradle the child's head, her lips are close to the baby's nose. It is an overwhelming visual sense of love. Gorman used as many techniques as he did materials to produce his art. His subject matter reflects his Navajo heritage. He believed that optimism is not all about happiness. It is knowing the sadness and the adversities of life while embracing the happiness that could easily evade us.

"What is with this guy's work that makes people weep publicly?" I wondered to myself.

Part of a great artist is the ability to portray the dynamic feelings of humanity, not the striped down feelings. R.C. Gorman brought nobility and tenderness through his dependable hand. He is the personification of the Navajo spirit; he is direct, lucid and simple. I kept looking at the people, amazed by how they were transfixed by the images. A group of women reflected on a piece named *Mystique*. They spoke about her staggering walk and the distinct powerfulness on her entire attitude.

"This is my favorite. I love the dynamic form of this woman," one of them said to her companions. "I want to copy this walk and the expression on her face," another exclaimed.

What people love about R.C. Gorman is that he allows them a glimpse of tenderness into his gentle spirit. He is one of a few to possess that strange power in his brush and express it through the spectacle of colors. What is also impressive about his work is that he seems to speak the language of all ages. His art is an amazing phenomenon which, I believe, will speak to many new generations throughout time. In *Navajo Woman,* her face is the most prominent image in the drawing. All other lines are not to be noticed as an exact form, but as a way to bring the eyes of the viewer to the face of the woman. Powerful strokes of a brush are no light matter. They move our feelings and help to distinguish the wonder of our deep self and lift our emotions.

During my interaction with the people milling around in the showroom, I recalled the patrons pondering: "Is his work unconventional?" I believe it is, because it reflects his Bohemian persona. "Is it paradoxical?" No doubt, because he himself is inexplicable.

There are no common words to describe any exceptional artists because, simply, most noted artists are eccentric.

The older couple was still sitting on the leather bench, staring at the image drifting to the sky. "I am curious, what is it about this painting that you've been staring at for a while?" I had to ask. She looked at me, her face full of kindness, and pain. "My husband is terminally ill. This is the image I'd like to have after he passes. He promises that he will be watching over me."

Art triggers memories and memories trigger emotions. And the cycle continues until it brings out our personal raw feelings, sometimes promising, sometimes despairing.

This sympathetic couple reminded me of an older Gorman black and white drawing of an aged Navajo couple. All lines are gently sweeping the background to encompass the full contentment of their eyes and their wrinkles. Their faces, full of happiness and strength dominate the canvas to reflect the bonding in their long life together. You are forced to smile at those two faces. You want to talk to them.

They are real. Just like that couple on the bench.

The rain subsided outside. It was getting late. A long drive to Scottsdale awaited me. I was certain that it was going to be a drive filled with emotions, feelings, and creative thoughts.

Jubilee

Navajo Mother In Supplication

Navajo Woman

Mystique

5

THE DEPTH OF HIS VISION

Arizona State College grew rapidly during the 1950's. It was established over fifty years earlier as a small school with a handful of students, but over time, expanded to the level that students could earn a master's degree in the arts and sciences. Due to the academic quality of their programs and the continued growth of students the school became Northern Arizona University in 1966.

R.C. enrolled briefly in Arizona State College before he interrupted his studies to join the Navy in 1951. The Navy provided the next installment in R.C.'s education: he enrolled in Guam Territorial College to study literature, intending to become a writer. During his time in the Navy, he earned money by sketching portraits of sailor's girls from photographs.

R.C. admired Peruvian-born Alberto Vargas who concentrated on painting women using watercolors and airbrush for a smooth effect. During Alberto's career, he worked with Ziegfeld Follies, Fox Movie Studios, Esquire and Playboy. He also painted mascots for units in the armed forces. Because of the nudity of his subjects, the nature and quality of his work caused controversy.

R.C. followed this path while in the Navy; he glamorized local girls for a small fee. Luckily, he soon realized that portraying woman for only their physical gifts was against his artistic beliefs.

After the Navy, in 1956, R.C. returned to Northern Arizona University in Flagstaff, where he majored in literature with a minor in art.

Jose Clemente Orozco, Diego Rivera and David Alfaro Siqueiros, are regarded to be Mexico's *Los Tres Grandes* muralists. These three artists revived the tradition of the Renaissance painting on large murals as meant to engage a wider viewing audience. Orozco, a politically committed artist, created an art form to promote the political causes of peasants and working people in the post-Mexican Revolution era.

R.C.'s love for the classical era of songs, literature and philosophy meant it was only natural to be attracted to Orozco's work, who was himself influenced by the greatness of Michelangelo's mannerism style and El Greco's distinctive visionary style. It is possible that once R.C. studied Orozco's work he felt a stronger connection to art and is the main reason he wanted to study in Mexico.

Gorman met with the tribal government and convinced them to finance his art studies in Mexico. He received the first scholarship ever given by the Navajo Tribal Council for study outside the United States. This trip was to change Gorman's artistic style forever and determine his fate as an artist.

In Mexico, he was introduced to the works of other giants of the arts who were not as well known outside Mexico to the general public as was Orozco. Besides *Los Tres Grandes* he was introduced to the work of Rufino Tamayo. Eventually all of these Mexican greats were recognized around the world for their use of color and freedom of style. R.C. never studied directly with them, but their influence on his art was tremendous. He was especially inspired by the vibrant colors which became an important component to R.C. Gorman's signature paintings. He also studied their abstract forms and shapes to create his incomparable realistic style and apply it with the same freedom when portraying his own people and traditions. During this time, the contemporary Native American art movement was nonexistent. Native American artists were confined to the traditional style. R.C. did not restricted himself to this style. He was unique and was always searching to improve his art.

The Mexican artists were a great influence to his art, but the person he admired growing up was his father. One of his favorite pastimes was to watch his father draw. He tried to imitate him by going outside to draw pictures on the earth. His first canvas was the rocks and the sand, first paintbrush was a pointed wooden stick and his first paint was the mud from the earth, sometimes red, other times brown. The times Rudy spent with his Dad were memorable; riding together on the Navajo mountains, branding cows in the ranch, being out in the fields in the beautiful open country. His father, Carl, was one of the first Native American artists to depart from tradition and paint from his own personal expression. Unfortunately, R.C. seldom saw his father during his early childhood because he was serving our country in World War II.

R.C.'s father gifted him the love of painting. The Mexican greats doubled his certitude to be an artist, but it was his grandmother and great grandmother who defined his art. They were the strong women who gave him life, confidence and inspiration.

R.C. Gorman was a pioneer artist in his generation. He did not concern himself with the glamorous look of a woman, like Vargas, but forever sought to capture their infinite inner beauty.

His grandmothers were his prototype of strong, earthy women. Their presence was powerful and gentle as they worked the earth and nurtured their children. They personified the Navajo women's spirit; remote and silent on the outside, forceful and divine in the inside.

They were the universal model of women in Gorman's eyes; it was a perpetual challenge to capture them on canvas.

As a boy, Rudy drew with charcoal on rocks and with a stick on the sand.

Later he made animals and Disney characters out of clay.

When he discovered pencils and paper, he began drawing in an unrestrained manner. Before he was ten-years old, he drew a naked woman; it was from the innocent eyes of a child but never-the-less, it brought a spanking from his teacher.

His personal force and originality in his painting matured from his themes of Navajo origins to an ongoing creative form and while moving farther away from the traditional images and techniques, he never lost the component of his Native American roots. His linear portrayal of the human figure, moving quietly among their chores, is unmatchable. Sure, the fact that he had very little while growing up on the the reservation seems harsh in today's society, but it was that simplicity that reflected on the entire body of his work.

It was that simplicity, coupled with his irrefutable talent, which propelled R. C. Gorman to be the most influential Native American artist.

6

GLORY AND TRAGEDY

There were several hard-fought battles before that iconic image of the war was broadcast across America; a handful of United States Marines raised the American flag on the top of Mount Suribachi, the highest point on the island of Iwo Jima.

The Navajo Code Talkers took part in some of the fiercest fighting with the Marines throughout the war against the Japanese. They were involved in the capture of Tarawa, a strategical base where they launched offensives further west to the key objectives of the islands of Guam, Saipan, and Tinian. The Navajo Code Talkers accurately directed naval and artillery gunfire during the Battle of Saipan.

In September 1944, the Marines began the landing on the beaches of Peleliu under heavy fire. It was a grueling battle that lasted over two months and both sides suffered heavy losses. For the Navajo Code Talkers, Peleliu was a harsh experience, being in the midst of an immense amount of artillery.

The next target was the island of Iwo Jima, a desolate island, but of a large strategic importance. Since Iwo Jima was Japanese territory, the Marines were aware that the Japanese would defend the island to their last man. The United States Navy, Army and Air Force relentlessly assaulted the island by air and sea for over eight months

On February 19, 1945, the Marines landed on Iwo Jima. They kept pushing forward as reinforcements kept landing on the beach despite the devastating enemy fire. The road to the victory was slow and painful. Over seventy thousand Marines had landed on Iwo Jima during the battle.

On February 23,1945, after four days of savage fighting, Mount Suribachi fell, ending with the iconic image of the Marines raising the United States flag over Iwo Jima. During the Battle for Mount Suribachi, the Navajo Code Talkers, using radios and walkie-talkies on the front lines, relayed coordinates of Japanese defenses to the Navy and Air Force. This directed the American firepower against enemy positions and, at the same time, coordinated the flow of troops, supplies, and equipment.

Thanks to the Code Talkers, air strikes and naval artillery pounded with accuracy the Suribachi's defenses.

The Navajo Code Talkers played a significant role in the battle of Iwo Jima. Their contribution was recognized by the United States Marines involved in the fight. One of the commanding officers, Major Connor stated, "Were it not for the Navajos, the Marines would never have taken Iwo Jima."

During that offensive push of the Marines, Carl Gorman became ill with malaria and was evacuated from Saipan to Pearl Harbor Medical Center for treatments. On September of 1945, the war was finally over and the Code Talkers returned to their homes. When Carl Gorman returned to the reservation, he learned that his wife was involved with another man. The marriage of Carl and Adele was over.

It was after the war that Carl Gorman rediscovered his love for painting. His work concentrated around the culture of his people and when he became successful, he never forgot his roots. Unemployment continued to be high on the reservation long after the war. He helped the poverty stricken people on the reservation by organizing shipments of food and clothing.

Mary Excie Wilson was born in Warren, Rhode Island. Because of her severe sinus infections, her father decided to take the family to the dry climate of the west to help his only child's health. After staying in several cities in Arizona and California because of his work, the Wilson family settled in Barstow, California. Mary's father, Clifford Wilson, was in charge of the Marine Corps supply base.

By this time, Carl Gorman had applied to a list of art schools and while waiting for replies, he got a job in the supply base that Clifford Wilson was in charge of. Wilson, impressed with Carl's work ethic, invited him to a Sunday dinner. Mary Excie, now a tall blond, met Carl for the first time at that Sunday dinner and discovered that they both had a common interest in the arts.

By now a skillful artist, Carl went away for further studies in the Otis Art Institute in Los Angeles for the next four years. As the years passed, Carl was enwrapped in his art and Mary was studying painting, nevertheless they kept in communication. Nine summers after they first met, Carl and Mary met again in Barstow. Mary was excited when Carl offered to give her instructions about her painting. After that summer they exchanged letters and bonded. The relationship grew stronger and despite her father's vehement objections, they got married in 1956. Carl was twenty years older than Mary.

Their first child Alfred Kee was born in 1957 and six years later they had their second child, Zonie.

Shortly after Kee stood on his feet, his father pushed him to be a painter. Kee was a natural. By the age of four he showed incredible talent and he even sold one of his paintings. Soon after, he sold a mosaic and at six he won first place for children in the Window Rock Fair. By the time he was eight, he was selling his work in galleries.

Meantime, in 1964, R.C. Gorman did several showings with his father to promote the new direction of Native American art. First was the *Father and Son Invitational Show* in Tulsa Oklahoma's Philbrook Art Center and later at the Heard Museum in Phoenix Arizona. It was headlined as *Gorman, a father and son rebels in Indian art.* It was a combined showing for varied media and material for which they were becoming noted and was praised for its diversity. The people who attended the show were captured by the rich and varied quality of the work. Their subject matter came from their

Navajo origins. The land and the culture from which they took pride. R.C. was thankful for the opportunity to be teamed up with his famous father.

Another "rebel" of the Gorman family was the young Kee Gorman, who at a very young age, showed signs of a unique talent.

Carl Gorman encouraged his son R.C. to be an artist and stressed the importance of finding his own inclinations. He was now taking the same approach with the young Kee; improve your techniques but explore uniqueness in style. Kee was headed for a promising career, his work was rapidly improving. Working alongside his Dad, he gained valuable knowledge.

Tragically, in the summer of 1966, on a family trip to Albuquerque, Mary, was driving with Carl in the passenger seat. The children Kee and Zonie were with Mary's mother in the back seat. Mary dozed off for a moment and the car veered out of control, spun off the pavement and rolled over a few times. All of the passengers were thrown out of the car. The children and grandmother were unconscious and taken first by an ambulance to the hospital in the nearest town of Grants, New Mexico. By the time they reached the hospital, Kee was dead. The ambulance returned to take Carl, who was in critical condition. Mother and daughter suffered minor injuries, but the grandmother died a few days later.

Kee was just nine years old.

7

THE DEFINING TRIP

The aftermath of foreign domination, dictatorship, political revolution and a civil war that ended on 1920, was still evidenced in Mexico during the decade of the forties. There was dreadful infrastructure, minimal tourism, and political confrontations which contributed to a chaotic social landscape.

Entering the decade of the fifties, the so-called time of *Mexican Renaissance*, there were signs of revival. The unity of the people came from an unexpected source. It wasn't the politicians or some miraculous social program designed to energize the people; it was the arts. Cultural influences and behavior changed as people gathered at various events and clustered in small groups, chatting and conversing with one another. Art created a sense of purpose and began to beautify the public spaces by providing venues for collective expression.

In the forefront of the *Mexican Renaissance* were the muralists. They instilled national pride to the wounded conscience of the people. Theirs was an art that was visual in the streets, the schoolyards, in the public buildings and reminded the people of the harsh past while inspiring them to reach for a brighter future. These images perched in the conscience of the people and played an important role in the rebirth of Mexican pride.

The ubiquity and high visibility of murals made public spaces an ideal canvas for those who wanted to get their message to the public. New public spaces were emerging in previously nonexistent locations and became more inviting and vibrant.

The outcome of the artistic movement of the muralists was such that it affected other creative components.

Mexican film production in the fifties reached its peak and experienced its greatest era, known as their Golden Age.

During that period, legendary singers surfaced. Some with their thunderous voices which expressed the pride of culture and others with smooth voices and romance drenched lyrics which composed eternal love songs to comfort the psyche of the war-worn people.

Novelists focused on realistic narratives and reached their peak while reflecting on self and national culture. Mexican literature blossomed to one of the most prolific and influential of the Spanish language. Octavio Paz was given the Nobel Prize for Literature, and legendary authors like Carlos Fuentes and Juan Rulfo, top the list of many highly respected Latin American writers.

Architecture began to show signs of Mexican personality and arts and crafts became a part of Mexico's identity.

The city of Guadalajara was one that experienced substantial growth after the end of the Mexican Revolution. This city became the hub of the Renaissance of Mexican art as more distinguished painters, poets, actors, writers and other representatives of the arts made it their home. It was the time that art started to shift from European influence to more Mexican themes.

During the decade of the fifties, art students were sent to Mexico from the United States and around the world, to study the painting style of the muralists.

This was also the time that defined R.C. Gorman's art.

It was on a trip with friends from San Francisco to Guadalajara that awakened unfamiliar images and a vast array of colors in Gorman's mind. There were open farmers markets with colorful fruits and flower shops on the streets with an abundance of gladiolus and other brilliant flowers. There were wandering singers walking into cantinas and mariachis serenading tourists. There were art stands selling handmade art and jewelry, kids playing soccer in the streets and barbers cutting people's hair under trees.

His first time in Mexico, Gorman saw a contrary lifestyle, yet with elements of familiarity with his own culture. For instance women washing clothes by the lake, grinding corn in the fields, getting water out of a well or embracing a child with love. But, what impressed R.C. the most, was the murals and their inescapable and overpowering city scenery.

When he walked into *Hospicio Cabañas*, a building to provide care and shelter for the handicapped, orphans and elderly, and saw Orozco's, *The Spanish Conquest of Mexico*, mural, portraying the history of Mexican people, it took his breath away.

Orozco's masterpiece is a conceptual assessment which represented Mexico's indigenous, the heroic conquest and the religious inspiration. R.C. stood for endless hours in awe admiring this complex achievement. This was his defining moment as he dreamed that he could do the same for his people. From that moment on, every other medium was slowly left behind and the signature R.C. Gorman style began to build wings. Rumors have it that when he left the building, his eyes were tearful. Jose Clemente Orozco, David Alfaro Siqueiros and Diego Rivera were trained in classical European techniques and their early works resemble European paintings styles. The current political situation in Mexico prompted these artists to break with European traditions and to start using bold native images, a plethora of bright colors and human activity. They became giants of the art and are known as *Los Tres Grandes*. Rivera spent considerable time in Europe on an art scholarship from the government. He studied around masters like Braque, Cezanne, and Picasso. In Italy, he studied the Renaissance and was introduced to fresco painting, a style important to a muralist. He began to emphasize the idea of popular art which all people could enjoy.

Rivera worked in a more traditional manner. He took his knowledge from European modernism and intermingled it with the art of old Mexico. The result was a new form that expressed his social and political ideas. He used bright colors and blended earthy shades to capture them in the vibrancy of his murals.

Orozco left Mexico because of the negative reaction from critics about his art. He spent time in the United States and Europe trying to define himself as an artist. In Europe, being fascinated by Byzantine mosaics and Greek mythology, he abandoned his usual historical subjects to portray, among other universal figures, the Titans and Prometheus in a human, fiery, superhero form. Orozco's fearless art, coupled with his unorthodox personality made him a national hero years later, upon his return to Mexico. The amazing fact about Orozco is that he created most of his art without his left hand. Early in his career, while in New York, he lost his left hand in a gunpowder accident.

The work of Orozco was somber and prophetic. He was not concerned with the past. He believed that the role of his artistic gift was to reach the people, to inspire and educate. Once Orozco committed himself to mural painting, he never went back to the easel.

Siqueiros, the youngest of the three, was sent to Europe on a scholarship to study art. In Paris, he met Diego Rivera, who urged the young painter to get in touch with his country's rich cultural past. Siqueiros work is recognized by his bold lines and exaggerated perspective. He masterfully integrated traditional art with innovative techniques. Most of his works involved his social concerns and reflects the revolutionary struggles. His style is vigorous with integrative movement, and his color range constricted to bring out dramatic, earthy effects. The result is powerful and spectacular.

The work of the three muralists was a collective effort. If one got an idea, they all integrated it. In spite of the close collaboration, the work of each man was very distinctive. Each painter was free to work in his own style and technique. Looking at the murals, it is easy to know which muralist painted what.

Though different in style and temperament, they were devoted to an art which they strongly believed was for the education and betterment of the people. *Los Tres Grandes* had a strong influence on how many artists perceived art in the twentieth century. There is no question that they also influenced the techniques and styles of future artists but also forced many to re-examine the role of art in society.

When R.C. returned from his trip to Mexico, he applied for a grant from the Navajo Tribal Council. He was awarded the first scholarship from the Navajo Nation to study art abroad. In Mexico, he spent a year living a Bohemian lifestyle while studying art and surrounded by individuals associated with strong social viewpoints. The unconventional way of life and the new school of thought re-energized him. The artists and poets he met in Mexico seemed eccentric to others, but their expressionism was aimed to shake the world and open its borders. For R.C., evoking the essence of the classical in music and philosophy, and being engulfed in spirituality was an experience that reminded him of his childhood and the way of life of his people.

The lifestyle of an avant-garde group of Mexican artists, as bohemian artists did since the nineteenth century in Europe, disturbed the high society's pretentious view of art. But it was that very lifestyle that liberated R.C.'s inner creative power, allowing him to leap onto life's pages in full color and propelling him to find R.C. Gorman.

While improving his oil painting skills, he experimented in drawing on butcher paper with a grease pencil and he worked on oily paper as well. Once the grease lines dissolved, it gave a washed effect to the images. While in Mexico, he was introduced to lithography, an artistic medium, a method of printing painted images from a stone's smooth surface. He mastered lithography later on in his life and used it throughout his career as a means of printing multiple original images of his paintings, as he did as a young boy, by drawing directly on the stones. He also experimented in using turpentine as a medium for added color and tried new images and different colors on screen-printing, pottery, masks, and textile.

The Mexican artists changed his way of expressing himself. He was captivated by the fact that these artists that he now admired were portraying realistic people and revealing earthy activity. Innovating ideas were always intoxicating for R.C. and now painting like a European seemed an old and overused style, but painting like a Mexican was exciting. The

Mexican images became Navajo subject matter, especially the women doing daily work seemed beautiful and meaningful to him. This new way of expressionism offered him a means of solace and spontaneity. His art was being reduced to brighter colors and a harmony of lines to balance the purity of his images. His hand was free and rhythmical, producing beautiful curves, moving to the tempo of a symphony conductor's baton. While classical music intensifies in his head, images were floating onto the canvas like beautiful notes. His work became a natural distance from reality, expressed with crispness and freedom. R.C. was not afraid to use brilliant colors to capture a mood rather than trying to depict reality. He emphasized the emotional power with sharp curved lines.

R.C. studied art at Mexico City College and lived with a nice Mexican family as a guest student. Staying with a host family was the best ways to get to know Mexican culture and truly experience the Mexican hospitality. It gave R.C. the comforts of independence and allowed him to focus on his art. In Mexican families, one must adapt to the rules and respect their customs. Mexicans value family hierarchy and parents are treated with a high level of respect. The families are usually large and there is a strong connection between family members, which includes extended family and close friends. Their holidays and festivals are celebrated with vigor and large gatherings.

It was in Mexico when R.C. began to paint nude models, usually female students in the City College. In his earlier work, nudes were a major subject.

Since the Classical Period of ancient Greece, a time when art reached new heights, through the Renaissance and the Neoclassical periods, the business of the artist was to find essences of beauty in surfaces.

It was the Fourth Century BC when Greek sculpture Praxiteles carved masterpieces like *Hermes* and *Aphrodite*, later renamed and painted as *Venus* by the great Botticelli. From Donatello to Michelangelo, Caravaggio, Picasso and other giants of the art, they created unclothed, priceless works of art.

In modern days, Western culture has determined that nudity in art is permissible. However, the religious perspective of morality portrays public nudity as disgraceful and pessimists renounce the beauty of the art, replacing with prejudiced visions.

While in Mexico, Rufino Tamayo, another Mexican artist had great influence on R.C. R.C.'s enchantment with Tamayo's work was the fact that he was portraying women in his paintings, showing their struggles through color choices and facial expressions. Tamayo's early works included many nudes, a subject which he eventually abandoned in his later career. Tamayo focused his composition as the focal point, rather than the subject alone. He believed that fewer and unique colors increase the possibilities to see the painting as a whole, a style that some critics disagree stating that fewer colors impoverish the images.

Tamayo's reaction against the political themes of the other Mexican muralists was not appreciated by his contemporaries. The importance of art addressing the societal injustices of the day, rather than the European styles such as Cubism and Surrealism, like Tamayo did, characterized him as a traitor to the political cause. Tamayo left the country to work in both the United States and France where he created many of his important works. Upon his return to Mexico, his work was received with high praise.

His rivalry with the main three Mexican muralists continued both in Mexico and internationally throughout his life. Some critics argued that he was worthy to be *The Fourth Great One* but this was a controversial subject.

Sitting in R.C. Gorman's Gallery in Scottsdale, I noticed the oddness of a couple that walked in. She was elegant and radiant and he was much older, ordinary and stern.

She walked slowly, examining every piece of art carefully, he was miserably uninterested.

Walking around the gallery, she was emotional and amazed – him; not that much.

"Astonishing" She said. "He is not original" he responded.

"Fabulous style," she murmured without looking at him - "I don't see it," he replied.

Eventually, he was tired of walking and complaining and sat across from me in the gallery's small sitting area.

He glanced at me, anxious to start a conversation, to speak his peace.

I remained silent. In cases like these, I let him take the lead initially to see what he wants to talk about.

There was a minute of silence. Outside the weather was glorious, one of those amazing Arizona days that inspires "Snowbirds" to flock to the Phoenix area in winter time.

"This, shopping for art, is torture," he said looking at me for a thoughtful gesture. I shook my head.

"Are you from around here?" he inquired.

"Yes, I live in Scottsdale".

"I am from Chicago," he continued.

I spent ten years in Chicago, but I do not share it with him since I don't want the conversation to take that direction. I was more curious about his low opinion of R.C. Gorman.

"Are you enjoying the weather here?" I asked.

"It's okay!"

I thought, does this guy have anything nice to say? "How about this art?", I asked.

"Nothing special, I hear that he paints like the Mexicans, like Zuniga."

And there it was; Francisco Zuniga. I wanted to tell him that Zuniga was not Mexican but Puerto Rican who migrated to Mexico later in life. His sculpture is what gave him fame and the only comparison with Gorman's paintings was that they both painted large people. Gorman painted strictly women, Zuniga both men and women, usually in the nude. The comparison of Zuniga with Gorman is like comparing Salvador Dali with El Greco. Although Zuniga's clothed women images are powerful, the choice of colors are soft grays, blues, and pink. His form is women sitting in a pyramid shape and the overall composition is calming. Most of his clothed women are wrapped in safety with a rebozo. Gorman's colors, on the other hand, are radiant; the women images project various activities and emotions.

If there were any comparison in styles, Gorman would be closer to Orozco, because of the color choices, than any of the others.

It was obvious that his information was baseless.

"Really? Do you think so?" I asked.

"Yeah".

"I haven't noticed."

"Believe me, it is true."

In a last effort, I downloaded one of Zuniga's most well-known pieces, *Chamulas Rojo*, on my phone and showed it to him.

"I do not see the resemblance," I said.

"What do you mean? Look. These big women!"

Well, I gave up. I smiled.

"What, you don't think so?" He insisted.

His wife finally walked up to us, to save me. "I got two pieces. Please pay," she told him.

He said nothing but just walked to the desk to give the clerk his credit card.

"Are we ready to go?" she asked.

"Yes dear."

I believe that everything we see, dream, imagine, read and hear stays hidden in our subconscious mind. If we refuse to reveal ourselves, if we are not willing to recount images that others have created, we will never grow. Ultimately, we can only be bonded with the reflection of our imagination, to find our way, to escape from the ordinary, to discover our reality and be able to correct, to re-create and to mold the unmatchable.

Marta

Daughter of the Moon

8

THE CULTURAL REVOLUTION

After Mexico, R.C. returned to San Francisco to find a city in transition. Unfamiliar scenes and chants filled the streets.

Peace. Baby. Peace.

Love. Not war.

Fists raised in indignation; Hell. No. We. Won't. Go.

Rainbows, Bandannas, Long Hair, Flowers, Peace Signs.

Dylan, Baez, Chaplin, Mitchell, leading the revolution with their voices.

"*If you're going to San Francisco, be sure to wear some flowers in your hair...*" had become the youth's anthem.

There was a shocking change from the conservative society, a society that just a short time ago, when Clark Gable said, "*...I don't give a damn!*" and the entire country gasped.

Not that long ago, Elvis' swiveling hips caused a massive disturbance around the country. The television cameras reveal him only from the waist up. The church warned, "Beware of Elvis Presley. He is possessed by the devil." The media was up in arms about the new phenomenon of animalism in music.

And now, a new social hostility was spreading not against one man but for an entire generation.

Let's not forget that a few years later, in a nation inflamed by prejudice, the groundbreaking film *"Guess Who's Coming to Dinner"* marked a defining moment of interracial relationships. It was a time when cinema was embracing realism with controversial subjects. Early in the film, a kiss between a Yale-educated black doctor and his white medical student fiancée, caused sleep anxiety to the conservative community.

Director Stanley Kramer's courageous challenge of an interracial relationship portrayed by Sidney Poitier and Katharine Houghton, could only have taken place in San Francisco.

The times were changing; there was freedom of expression, people were not afraid to vocalize, inspired to protest without the chains of social shame.

And then...and then, no longer the index finger is pressed against the lips for silencing the voices.

People were free to talk, to revolt, to create. Zeal and idealism overcame fear and silence.

Artists inspired with freedom of expression began to fill their canvas with images that not too long ago would have cause social scrutiny.

San Francisco, along with New York and Los Angeles, was becoming the epicenter of new arts.

Abstract Expressionism was scattering to the west from New York. The art was heavily criticized by most critics and the artist's credibility was rejected.

Abstract artists in lower Manhattan, following the footsteps of Pollock, Rothko and de Kooning, removed this art from the fringe to add another dimension in the western art world. Art did not escape the wave of radicalism in the sixties. Undoubtedly, Andy Warhol opened the curtains of the modern art stage to Pop Art. While Pop Art was breaking down the social parameters, there were other flashing points in art concepts, like Minimalism and Conceptualism that carved out a new space for art's general definition.

This was the time that the art of R.C. Gorman was evolving in San Francisco, a Nirvana for artistic expressions. Now, in his early twenties, young, good looking and ambitious, he was energized to advance his art to new expressionisms.

Mexico offered him solace and spontaneity, but San Francisco liberated his creativity.

The Mexican artists changed the ways of expressing himself and San Francisco was the place that allowed him to express himself freely.

R.C. took art classes at San Francisco State University. To get out of the "starving artist" level and help with school expenses, he worked the graveyard shift at the post office, sorting mail.

He also modeled for art classes in colleges and private art studios, a job that turned out to be the catalyst for his growth as an artist. The education of being a model was invaluable. While he stood on the pedestal, he listened to the lectures of the best art teachers in the bay areas and heard the student's feedback. He absorbed the knowledge of several masters as he was getting paid, and learned as he sat at the lecture.

In San Francisco, R.C. lived and painted on the upper floor of an old Victorian house. The house, in a quiet neighborhood at the top of the hill on Army Street, was a perfect hideaway. His constant companions were his cats and his favored pastime was cooking. R.C. developed the love of cooking as he was forced to prepare food for himself, at first to save money. Eventually, he was captivated with the chemistry of food ingredients and began to create his own recipes – a parallel to his fascination with the chemistry of colors. He grew herbs and flowers on his balcony, where he spent much time overlooking the city.

During the day, he painted. In the evenings he usually walked, and sometimes rode the trolleys to visit the galleries in Upper Market Street, to read in the San Francisco Public Library or go to his work. All of these places were around the perimeter of a few miles. His work in the Post Office was tedious, but the building was an exciting place and was reminiscent of his time in Mexico.

The building of the Rincon Annex Post Office is now classified as a historic building and one of the major destination for art lovers visiting San Francisco. The interior of the Rincon Center building, then San Francisco's busiest post office, featured several life-size murals, painted by Anton Refregier. The social realism style murals, completed right after World War II, generated fierce controversies both for the artistic style and political message. In the end, however, the art community, progressive politicians, and large crowds of protesters rallied on behalf of the murals. So the murals remained. The murals in Rincon Center reflect the character of the city and the immense changes in political and social life throughout the decades.

R.C. was a loner at home; he treasured his privacy but, when around people, he exhumed his charismatic personality and the passion for his art

During his alone times, he experimented with various mediums. He went through a landscape period, integrating mountains, rivers and forests with people. Then it was a contemporary approach to surrealistic style. Even though surrealism unlocked the power of his imagination, this style was left behind. He did abstract expressionism, a style that allowed him to express his emotions, but he was not done searching. There was pottery, rugs, masks, clowns, nudes; everything was to be tested while searching for a style that would guide him to clarity of his artistic vision.

He liked to work with oil because it is smooth like cream, he could manipulate it, tell it what to do. He worked with acrylic, even though it has a mind of its own, he challenged himself to tame it. He wanted to develop a new approach handling these colors. First, he tested the impasto approach. The impasto technique is to apply paint to the canvas as thickly as possible. The lavishly textured and the three-dimensional surface could create dramatic visual effects. And then, he tried a very watery approach. Eventually, he developed his binding approach of color bits. Color design is used by following one's artistic judgment. The concept of color harmony is to view the colors and for the artist to decide whether color combinations are in visual harmony. For R.C., color harmony was essential to develop his rug series.

Color harmony was also important for his pottery series. To age the pottery, he wet it with plenty of water and then tossed sand on it. Even though acrylic is probably the most versatile of paints, achieving color harmony painting with acrylic could be tricky because the color changes slightly when drying.

During his first few years in San Francisco, R.C. made frantic efforts on various mediums and techniques. But, the things he seems to love doing most were rug and pottery motifs. It was the abstract canvases based on Navajo rug designs and Pueblo pottery patterns that brought him first recognition.

It seemed that the Navajo reservation was his source of inspiration. Whatever medium he worked with, he still retained his Native American feeling.

In San Francisco, R.C. Gorman's artistic output was colossal. However, most of the work he did back then was sold, given away or painted over.

R.C. Gorman built a bridge, for himself and other artists, between the traditional and the contemporary style of Native American art, the two cultures in which he lived.

His confidence about his art coupled with his polite demeanor projected a certain charm; it was effortless for him to make friends. He befriended several gallery owners and the group of his artist friends was growing.

At a time of no Internet, email, Facebook or Twitter, new painters, writers and musicians depended on individual appearances, personal interactions, artist's clubs, and word-of-mouth, to reach the locals, before expanding to a wider audience via print and radio.

R.C. Gorman worked tirelessly to produce his art and to build a business network. This was a difficult task in a city full of artists. He had already assembled a small base of customers, but he needed a showing to raise his status to a credible artist.

The owner of a coffee gallery on Grant Street, an older gentleman who liked to give the floor to young artists, gave R.C. Gorman his first exhibition. Although his art was exceptional, it was by no means unique. He was doing the same kind of art everyone was doing in San Francisco in those days, with the exception of a few Native American women.

R.C. has always observed and learned, a gift from his days as a model and, when some of his first collectors encouraged him to paint more Native American women, he listened. After his first exhibition, he was excited when the gallery started handling his work. Unfortunately, the gallery closed its doors when the owner had a heart-attack and died.

During the exhibition, Charles and Ruth de Young Elkus, major collectors of Native American art, were impressed with this young artist's work. Charles de Young Elkus was an attorney. The couple was acknowledged by their efforts to help the Native American tribes with their many rights.

R.C. Gorman's career started to solidify; he was now doing exhibitions and competed successfully in Native American art competitions, bringing home first place awards.

His first opportunity to expand his art nationally came when one of his art collectors contacted The Philbrook Museum and Art Center in Tulsa, Oklahoma. He was included in the biographical directory of American Indian painters.

His oil painting titled "*Desert Mother*" won first place and his lithograph "*Navajo Mother in Supplication*" won second place.

Jeanne Snodgrass, director of the museum, became a big fan and helped him with more exhibits.

Desert Mother

Mother and Child

While in Oklahoma, he met with a group of artists from Houston who encouraged him to visit the art community in Houston. R.C. did visit Houston and stayed there for a short period, but he was not convinced that Houston was the place to grow as an artist. He returned to San Francisco bonded with a life-long friendship with the Houston artists.

R.C. was on his way to Gallup, New Mexico to meet his artist friend, Barry Tinkler, who was coming from Houston. Their final destination: the city of Taos.

The heavy commute traffic was left behind as the train was stretching beyond the sea-bound hills of San Francisco Bay, and into the celebrated scenery of Northern California. The morning rain had subsided; clear skies have replaced the melancholic feeling. Passing between the Santa Cruz mountains, the scenery was shifting from green rolling hills to flat fields, and then into the great agricultural valleys. Throughout this long stretch, looking out of the window, there were vineyards, strawberry fields, garlic fields, artichokes and lettuce. There were teams of pickers frantically packaging vegetables to supply the markets.

Before reaching Salinas, the three hour ride in Monterey County had gone by unnoticed. In this epic land, a solid agriculture area of Northern California, the train was winding quickly through farms, flat fields, quiet pastures and horse ranches.

As the train was rumbling by the agricultural lands extended along the Salinas River, his eyes were yearning for more colorful landscapes.

The gleaming sun enhanced the already radiant colors of the earth. Soon there were meadows covered with bright orange California poppies, an impressive floral display, especially when they ascent to high hillsides and blend with lilies and other blue and yellow wildflowers.

Into San Luis Obispo County, the train glides through green vineyards and winds around horseshoe curves that allowed him to see the scenery in different dimensions, then slowly, leaving the inland, aiming towards the coastlines.

The scenery remained impressive; the sky seemed bluer while moving into Central California and approaching the magnificent coast from San Luis Obispo, before reaching Santa Barbara. As the train hugged the coast for more than one hundred miles, passing Pismo Beach and Point Conception, he wished that the train could slow down, to see everything in slow motion. On the one side in the background the rocky scenes of the Santa Ynez Mountains, the dramatic coastal scenery below on the other side, and the poppy fields in between; this land was breathtaking.

This coastline south of Pismo Beach, all the way up to Big Sur, is what people come to California to see.

Hugging the Pacific coast, the train continued toward Santa Barbara, now trading in the green valleys for majestic waves crashing on the rocks and then the flat beaches of Santa Barbara. This is one of the most spectacular sequences of scenery.

The afternoon sun, followed the train throughout the day, started tilting into the far horizon. By the time the train passed Ventura, darkness had enveloped it. It was timely because there wasn't much to see beyond this point. R.C. closed his eyes; there was so much scenery, so many colors to be preserved in his mind. He smiled as the unique rhythmic sound of the train lulled him to sleep.

The sudden stop of the train awakened him. They have arrived at the Los Angeles Union Passenger Terminal in downtown Los Angeles.

After a lengthy stop at the Los Angeles Union Passenger Terminal to exchange passengers, today known as Union Station, the train headed eastwards.

In his roomette, R.C. folded down his bench seat into a bed and tried to get some sleep. Since there were not enough passengers, he did not have to share his narrow room.

The bright lights of Los Angeles plummeted into darkness as the train moved eastward, only to briefly reappear as they passed Riverside, San Bernardino and Barstow. There was a long way to go, but R.C.'s sleep was often interrupted by nostalgia as the train was approaching familiar territories. Entering Arizona land, passing Kingman and coming to Flagstaff, the nostalgia intensified. Flagstaff is a special place for him; it was his first college experience. Just a few hours northeast was the Canyon de Chelly. Memories of his childhood and celebration of his culture awaken strong yearnings.

On the eastern horizon, the first orange rays of the sun peeked over the snow-covered mountain peaks soaring above Flagstaff.

Moving beyond the depot revealed Flagstaff, a city enclosed by ponderosa pine forests, ageless Aspen, Juniper and Fir trees. A transparent haze blanketed the mountaintops, towering over the dense forests, protecting the hidden wildlife. It was a dramatic landscape of this scenic wonderland.

R.C. opened his window to breathe the crisp air of his ancestors, as the train entered the ghost town of Canyon Diablo, travelled into the Navajo Nation land and then beyond Winslow into New Mexico. The high desert of New Mexico is the definition of the American Southwest. Along the way of this rugged desert are red rock mesas, massive limestone arches, outback mountain vistas, sandy dunes and canyons.

Approaching Gallup, the rugged desert mostly vanishes and becomes a scenic desert, replaced largely by mountain ranges, enveloped in pine forests and surrounded by meadows. Finally, the train reached its destination.

By the time R.C. met his friend, it was late afternoon.

9

THE RISE OF GORMANISM

In the summer of 1966, after the automobile accident, times were difficult for the Gorman family. They were dealing with their father's health and the loss of young Kee. Carl was severely depressed after his son's death and vowed that he would never paint again. In addition to the great physical pain he endured during his lengthy recovery, he was suffering from extreme emotional pain. The doctors expressed concern that he may never walk again. However, after two months in the hospital, he walked out using crutches, then with a cane and soon after he walked free of any support. R.C. visited his father after his discharge in Window Rock and stood by his father's bedside for endless hours. Sometimes he brought along some of Carl's old paintings to motivate him to start working with his brush again. Other times he brought pencils and papers and by drawing in front of his Dad, he was hoping that his Dad would take the pencil away to correct the lines as he did when Rudy was a child.

"Come on, Dad, let's work on something new. I'd love to do another show together," he would say.

But there was nothing that could change his father's mind; the brush and the pencils reminded him of Kee, standing beside him, painting together

R.C. was devastated to see his hero devoid of spirit, fading away.

Finally, at age sixty, several years after the accident, Carl Gorman returned to painting and before his death at ninety-years-old he produced some of his most important work.

During the year of his father's health struggle, R.C.'s art production was almost non-existent. It was one of the few times in his career that he painted stark and painful images which reflected his feelings. One of these was a series of darkly-themed paintings for which he called *The Enigma Suite.*

When unable to understand the alarming attacks of anxiety through common sense, artists have always used their art as a reminder of the ephemeral human struggle to interpret pain. The macabre subject matter is not only symbolic in art images, but it is quite literal a representation of the written and spoken word. Many great artists and intellectuals have used grim references of life's suffering to understand what it means to be human, and others to adopt the darkening subject as their art medium.

Most great artists like Van Gogh, Picasso, even Rembrandt periodically created unsettling works. Other morbid artists have permanently crossed the line from grievous to gruesome. Only a few, like Monet, escaped that trend and chose to forever stay with the beauty of the soul.

We see the same trend in classical music, especially with Beethoven and Brahms and in theater - mostly in opera. However, the definition of living and dying is more realistic in literature than any other art form. We find morbid trends in the works of Virginia Woolf or Nietzsche among the many famous authors who were big fans of dark romanticism.

In modern literature, there is a thin line between horror and morbid. Horror can be a natural human emotion while being permanently morbid is mentally unhealthy. It takes the brilliance of the poet to create a balance between the strange union of beauty and pain, to grasp the perplexed unfamiliarity of life and the mystery of suffering. Such tragic poets were Aeschylus, Sophocles, Euripides and, later on, Shakespeare, Schopenhauer and Edgar Allan Poe.

However, the definition of living and dying is more realistic in classical literature.

Plato's *Phaedo* is one of the best examples of lessons for hoping that death is not in vain. In *Phaedo*, just before his death, Socrates introduced the logic that dying is nothing else but being dead. He then pursues the argument to prove the immortality of the soul. Following the Socratic thought, the Stoic philosophers believed that unhappiness is the result of human ignorance and if someone is unkind it is because he is unaware of his universal reason to be. In order to develop self-control and overcome destructive emotions like anger, resentment, jealousy and fear, you must understand suffering and death.

It is safe to say that Gorman was not a fan of dark doctrines or morbid subjects. The central thought of Gorman's art evolved from his studies of classical philosophy, inspirational music, his love for nature and thought-provoking human expression. His struggle with death was a transient one, and the legions of his fans are thankful for it because he has given the world an art of vivid expressionism for an imaginary utopia and not the morbid cacophony of gloomy forthcomings.

The Enigma Suite was an essential grieving to help him understand that human sorrow is a journey that we all must take in life. Looking at one of the pieces in *The Enigma Suite* called *Night II*, one would see the tormenting mother's face while leaning her head on a younger woman's shoulder for comfort. The younger woman is staring into the darkness searching for hope; the expression on her face is stern as if she is wanting to see beyond the darkness. In another piece of *The Night Series*, the focal points of a crouching young girl are the hands and the face. Her sharp fingernails resemble hooks. One hand is grasping the ground as if to dig into it, while the other hand is embracing her body, as if to protect it. The expression on her face appears to be a wondering of what is beyond the surface of the earth.

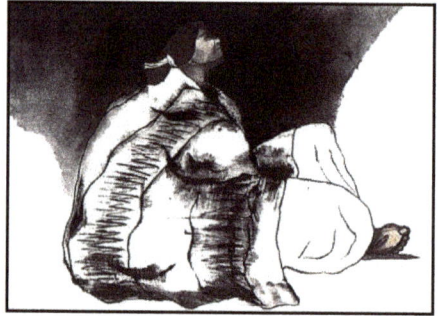

Over two years later, when R.C. traveled to New Mexico to meet up with his friend Barry Tinkler, the artist from Houston, he was back to his old self. His creativeness, optimism and classical music returned home.

The two friends, after catching up over dinner, took the bus to Taos.

R.C. and Barry arrived in Taos at night. The town was wrapped in muted darkness, not a soul on the streets. The moon was hidden behind the clouds and, other than a few meager lights, there was no indication of life. The winter was about to start and, at this higher altitude, there was a noticeable coolness in the air. The rumor was that this was a great artist town but so far, being their first time here, they were not impressed.

The two friends walked towards the lights of a motel sign.

The sun slowly came out in the morning, casting its first meager beams of light across the mountains and, as it drifted beyond the mountaintops, it revealed a different city. When the two friends stepped out from their motel, they felt the crispness of a soft, whispering air and saw a charming city surrounded by rolling mountains.

The town was slowly waking up; there were a few cars in the streets and smells of breakfast foods were coming from nearby. They walked by the small plaza and onto the streets to find a quaint town, brimming with galleries and a variety of boutiques.

They roamed around talking to business owners and introducing themselves to other artists. They received mixed messages about the town's activity. Some people encourage them to stay while others complained about tourism and lack of business. To them, the gallery visitors seemed sporadic, perhaps because they were used to the frantic lifestyle of the big cities.

"Why so few people?" they would ask.

"The busy art season is about over." Would be the common answer.

In this culture-rich city, the waves of art enthusiasts slowdown in September. There are occasional visitors from the nearby cities for various festivals. Nature lovers come in the fall to see the cottonwoods turning from green to yellow, and later on, the winter skiers flock the city to ski on the surrounding mountain slopes.

After an exhausting walk, visiting just about every gallery throughout the day, gallery owners had rejected their request to display their art.

Taos and art have an unusual relationship which has gone through transformations since the early 1900's when American and European artists turned Taos into the center of Native American based art themes. But, as new artists were flocking the city, eventually the art focus turned to classic western landscapes. Eventually, as the excitement of the early days wore off, there was nothing fascinating to draw art lovers to the city. That was until a group of modern artists came to Taos in the 1940's and transformed the city into a hotbed of contemporary art. After the movement of contemporary art subsided, Taos became a predominantly western art center.

By the time R.C. was looking for a gallery to handle his art, the art galleries in Santa Fe and Taos were back to a more romantic classic western style themes. Even though some of the galleries welcomed traditional Native American art; this kind of art was not prioritized. Especially at this time when Taos had lost its luster and gallery owners reserved their wall space for popular art and name-recognition artists.

When R.C. presented his portfolio, most of the gallery owners didn't know what to do with it. Some said, "If you want to be successful here you have to walk the walk and do what sells." But Gorman was determined to push the envelope, unwilling to compromise his artistic integrity. One of the last stops for the two friends, was the Manchester Gallery, a stop that proved to be the cornerstone of R.C. Gorman's career.

John Manchester, the owner of the gallery, looking at Gorman's portfolio, saw something in Gorman's work that others didn't see, and asked for time to talk to his partner.

Barry Tinker felt that this city was not for him and returned to Houston, but R.C. stayed. There was an inexplicable energy keeping him there.

John Manchester's partner was Lady Dorothy Brett, a British aristocrat, who along with D.H. and Frieda Lawrence, were searching for the ideal place to create a utopia society, which they called it *Rananim*. She fell in love with the land and its people and moved permanently to Taos in 1924 to focus on her art. She invited several famous artists of the time to join them, adopting a Bohemian lifestyle and creating their art in the inspiring surroundings of the natural world away from the artificial city life.

The two partners were impressed with Gorman's work and agreed to give him a one-man exhibition. His first presentation at the Manchester Gallery was extremely successful and Mr. Manchester decided to bring R.C. Gorman back for two more shows.

R.C. returned to San Francisco and shared his time between the two cities. The next shows in the Manchester Gallery were sold out. The name R. C. Gorman was now buzzing around Taos. Other Galleries in town asked to handle his work, but he refused, staying loyal to John Manchester whom R.C. adopted as his mentor and treated him with the respect reserved for a father.

R.C. worked tirelessly to improve his art in all mediums. He was forever asking and learning. The one medium that he always wanted to master was lithography but, since he has seen the best, he refused to study with anyone else. The best, according to him, was an older Mexican artist named Raul Anguiano whom he met while R.C. was a student in Mexico.

Besides Taos, R.C. Gorman was now showing in Scottsdale's Art Wagon Gallery. R.C. and Anguiano reconnected in Scottsdale.

"If you want to learn lithography, you must learn from the best master printer there is, and the best is Jose Sanchez in Mexico City," Anguiano told him.

Under the guidance of Jose Sanchez, R.C. learned how to use a greasy medium, usually, pencils or crayons washed in oil, to draw images on a specially prepared flat limestone. Lithography printing is based on the principle that oil and water do not mix. A solution of gum arabic is applied to the stone to combine with the greasy particles and enhance the image. Then the artist sponges the stone with waters and uses a hand-roller to apply the ink to the stone. The ink adheres only to the image drawn with the pencil and is repelled by the water. This process is repeated several times until the image is ready to print. When ready, the paper is placed on top of the stone and run through a hand press. Lithography printing is both precise work and intense labor.

Studying under Jose Sanchez in Mexico City, between R.C.'s limited Spanish and Jose's few words of English, they somehow communicated and R.C. came back home understanding lithography. With the knowledge of lithography, he completed his quest to master all medium and he was now ready to move permanently to Taos.

He used lithography throughout his life as a means of printing original multiple images of his ideas. The process reminded him of the days when he was a young boy and drew images on stones. His most prolific production of lithography was in the mid-seventies. At the same time, R.C. Gorman was casting bronze; another highly difficult process. First, the artist must create a clay sculpture that is completely smooth. This was another reminder of his childhood when he was making mud figures while herding sheep with his family. From the clay sculpture, a mold is made to cast the bronze artifact.

By 1968 his art was selling well and, when Mr. Manchester gave him the opportunity to buy the gallery, R.C. did not think twice. He borrowed money from his family and the Manchester Gallery became the Navajo Gallery. This was the first Indian-owned art gallery in the United States. Having his gallery was a new milestone – but now what?

In his excitement to have his gallery, the impulsive, artistic mind overruled long-term financial planning. However, he quickly realized that if his novel idea was to becomes a reality and if his long-term vision was to survive, it could only be accomplished with strong work ethics and a mission-driven belief.

R. C. Gorman believed in his ability and failure was not an option.

He was aware that eventually he would come to crossroads with his business and was willing to seek his answers through trial and error. The important thing at first was to reveal to the world the images he had conceived in his mind. Primarily his iconic imagery of Navajo women.

However, at this major crossroad of Gorman's life, the eternal question remains; "What is the artist's definition of success?"

The true artist thinks about art at every waking moment, they go to sleep thinking and dreaming about art. Most serious artists have strong work ethics, knowing that success could only be achieved through perseverance.

But, to be successful, they must understand the entrepreneurial aspects of making a living. It is best to delegate the business tasks to supportive people who value their relationship and to limit their time of emotional involvement with people who are negative.

The definition of success to a true artist is a moving target; a lifelong pursuit of an unreachable perfection.

The space became his home, studio, and gallery, where he personally dealt with the growing numbers of other artists he was helping and with the public that walked in. He was sleeping on a cot, and was at work by sunrise, working intensely, eating a moderate lunch and back to work.

Taos is a town with a colorful history, and as is the case with every old town, there is no escape from the subject of the supernatural. There are plenty of stories about ghost sighting around town. The places where strange occurrences have been reported are the usual suspects; Museums, old estates, historic hotels and naturally, unmarked graves in the cemetery. Most of the city's famous residents have now become ghosts. The rumors included the Manchester Gallery which had its own ghost, none other than Mabel Dodge Luhan.

For an artist living in his workplace, the scents of oil paints, linseed oil and lanolin overtook the home. Easels and piles of canvases consumed all living space. The decorations are brushes, drawing pencils and palette knives. There was always excitement in the morning when the large window let the sunlight in.

The recruiting of trusted friends began when Ella, an inspiring young Navajo artist, walked into the gallery for a quick visit. Several hours later she was still there, talking to R.C. about the Navajo life, about art, about the future and before leaving she agreed to take a job as a hostess. The business could not afford a salary for her, but she was happy to live in the upstairs part of the gallery, travel periodically with R.C. and watch him paint.

In his quest to help new artists he eventually took on over fifty artists to promote their work. Unfortunately, they did not sell well and, while his personal production was in demand, it became apparent that the gallery should be a showcase for R.C. Gorman alone. Gorman liked to work with a live model, usually a friend.

A few weeks after Ella started working in the gallery, a young man named Curtis, himself a young artists, walked into the gallery. He was hired as a studio assistant to help with R.C.'s work, to stretch canvases, deliver artwork and to be the point of contact between R.C. and the outside world.

Another day a young lady walked in the gallery and said, "Hello my name is Virginia would you like some lunch?" She was a music teacher and for additional income, she was selling sandwiches to businesses. Like so many people that walked in the Navajo Gallery, she was at once captivated by Gorman's charismatic personality and the uniqueness of his art. So, Virginia Dooley, who walked into the gallery to sell a sandwich spent the next thirty-some years with her name becoming synonymous with the R.C. Gorman legacy.

Lady Dorothy

10

TAOS, A REFUGE FOR ARTISTS

"What is so special about this land that attracts people who are seeking an escape from the city noise?"

"Why do creative minds and nature lovers make this their ultimate dwelling place?" These are among the questions people have been asking about the art magnetism of Taos. The simple answer; it is the landscape.

It is the main reason that Taos attracted artists of all mediums since the late 1800's, a time when artists and writers were seeking to capture the remaining vestiges of the Old West before it disappeared into tall buildings and highways.

At first, Phillips and Blumenschein, two New York artists who were inspired by the rugged land and the impressive light of the area, made Taos their permanent home.

In their desire to establish an American artist colony in Taos they invited other American artists to join them. Among them E.I. Couse who achieved fame for painting about the lives and culture of the indigenous people of New Mexico. Also, Oscar Berninghaus, known for his paintings of Native Americans, Cowboys, and ranch life. Additionally were painters, Herbert Dunton and Joseph Henry Sharp who President Theodore Roosevelt commissioned to paint the portraits of two hundred Native American warriors who survived the Battle of the Little Bighorn.

More and more artists joined the *Taos Society of Artists*. The main purpose of the six original members was to promote the sale of their work, create exhibitions of their paintings across the country and finally promoting Taos as an important art colony.

It was a woman who was responsible for expanding the Taos art colony by bringing famous artists, writers, and other celebrities to Taos.

Heiress, art sponsor, and writer Mabel Dodge Sterne planned only a brief vacation to New Mexico but was infatuated with the magnificent landscape and the modest small town so she moved permanently to Taos. Another reason for moving to Taos was Tony Lujan, a Taos Pueblo Native American whom she fell in love with and married.

On a twelve-acre land with the unspoiled views of the Taos Mountains, the two newlyweds built an impressive estate of six houses, orchards, barns and stables. The property is known as *Los Gallos Estate*. Mabel Dodge Luhan invited many artists and writers to Taos and as more flocked the city, it was necessary to build a large guest house, known as *Hacienda del Sol*, for their many guests. The rooms of the hacienda were once occupied by D.H. Lawrence and his wife Frieda, Georgia O'Keefe, and Ansel Adams.

D.H. Lawrence was the ultimate spokesperson for this new movement in art.

Georgia O'Keeffe in her painting "*The Lawrence Tree*" immortalized the pine tree under which Lawrence wrote. It was there where Lawrence was inspired to take up painting. Later on, Lawrence attempted to exhibit his paintings in London, but the show was shut down on the grounds of obscenity. Since Lawrence was a *persona non grata* because of his notorious book "*Lady Chatterley's Lover*" the paintings were confiscated to be destroyed but ultimately were saved when Lawrence promised to remove them from Great Britain soil. He brought them back to Taos and most of these paintings are displayed in the La Fonda Hotel on the Taos Plaza. Eventually, the era of romanticism came to an end. After a dismal period, a group of American modernists, known as the *Taos Moderns*, arrived in town from New York and San Francisco to revive the art scene. Like earlier artists, they portrayed the colorful landscape and cultural influences but captured the abstract essence of a subject, rather than the realistic images.

The peak of the modernists was short-live and Taos tourism slowed down again until two freewheeling bikers rolled into town. The two bikers speeding on the open highway surrounded by the beautiful landscape and wrapped under the Steppenwolf classic sound, "....*Get your motor runnin'- Head out on the highway - Lookin' for adventure - And whatever comes our way...*" The landmark film *Easy Rider,* with Peter Fonda and Dennis Hopper, was a generational touchstone; it captured the imagination of anyone who yearned to run free. The movie was mostly filmed around the Taos area. One of the stars, Dennis Hopper, bought the Mabel Dodge Luhan's, *Hacienda del Sol* and stayed there for a couple of decades. After the movie, tourism showed a sharp but temporary increase. The visitors that flocked to the city were not as much art lovers but motorcycle groups, environmentalists, hitchhikers, and people who arrived on psychedelically painted Volkswagen buses. It was a passing trend. The climate in Taos was too cold for bikers and hipsters who, after the first signs of cold weather, returned to the familiar grounds of California.

And then it was quiet once again.

Before arriving in Taos R.C. Gorman, now approaching forty years of age, was ready to endure whatever obstacle in order to reach the pinnacle of his artistic career. Since he was a child his restless energy needed an outlet and found it in a purpose and a vision for the future, a vision that helped him overcome adversities. The fact that he was born in poverty and endured a prejudice society did not taint his love for the art.

He was rapidly becoming the town's celebrity but that was not enough. He wanted the world to know his art.

Opening his gallery, at first, he had to endure the difficult financial times. Gorman pawned his few valuable things to keep the gallery's door open. At first, he didn't even own a car, in fact, he didn't know how to drive.

While growing up, he was told the story of surviving death. His mother was in labor with him for over twenty hours, baby Rudy was born premature and was placed in an incubator. The doctor told the family that it would be a miracle if the baby survived.

In the Navajo culture, the one person you never disobey is your grandmother and when Rudy's great grandmother asked the family to take the baby out of the hospital and bring him home, it was not a request. She even walked into the hospital, demanding the baby's release to make sure that he came home immediately. The baby was brought home and she saved Rudy by nursing him with goat's milk and coffee.

The story of his near death was told to him enough times to double his certitude that life is precious. If you could imagine yourself teetering on the edge of life and death, the meaning of survival takes on a different perspective. There is a spirit that evaluates the pinnacle of life, one that contradicts adversities, especially for an artist who lives with the irresistible impulse of creativeness.

R.C.'s life now revolved around the gallery. He loved hosting parties, he would walk in the plaza and invite everyone to his birthday parties. He was willing to support exhibitions by other artists and he would always try to show up for his friend's celebrations.

The operation of the Navajo Gallery was unorthodox, none of the business-as-usual art gallery formulation applied. There was no elevator music, pretentious kindness or any of the "salesperson" approach to buying art. R.C. Gorman's gallery hours changed according to his schedule, a flexibility suitable to his free-spirited personality. Anyone walking in the gallery could easily be invited to dinner, asked to pose as a model, buy a painting, play with his pet pig or step around his pet iguana. If he wasn't painting, he would gladly take people back to his garden to show them the growing vegetables and herbs. Visitors often encountered him working at his easel and his model posing for his latest drawing. The reason that so few early studio drawings exist is that people waited for him to finish the piece and bought it right off the easel.

Ledoux Street hadn't been discovered yet, but due to the imaginative approach to running an art gallery, Gorman was putting it on the map.

Ledoux Street, when the Navajo Gallery was founded was more like a back alley, about a block-long dirt path, a residential area with a row of tiny houses lining the street. There was not even a street sign nor street lights, and there was no parking other than a small driveway, but people somehow found their way to the gallery. The visitor had to walk the long dirt path, search for the entrance to the driveway, see the gallery window, pass under the low archway and into the courtyard, before finding the door to enter into an amazingly spacious gallery.

As the word about R.C. Gorman was spreading beyond Taos, there was increased foot traffic around the area of the Navajo Gallery. People were roaming around, confused and trying to find the gallery. "Where is R.C. Gorman's Navajo Gallery?" was a common question from the visitors.

One of Gorman's great abilities was to be able to portray a model's personality on canvas. The live models Gorman used were usually people that he knew well. In fact, some of the regular models continuously posed for him for many years. The familiarity of the model was a source of an emotional inspiration and helped him with a better orientation on his subject. Some of the women he painted were of Spanish and Oriental descent, but most of his models lived in the Native American community of Taos Pueblo.

Modeling for R.C. Gorman was not for those who were sensitive about their bodies, nor was it necessary for them to have the perfect figures. Gorman was interested in emotions, and he preferred models who have full bodies, it was his charming personality and the skillful strokes of his brush that made them feel beautiful.

As the demand for his art was exploding, he was searching for a supportive cast. It was essential for him to be with individuals he could trust, not only to help manage the business but to become a part of his life. His requirements were simple; he wanted people with the potential of staying with him for a long time and would cultivate a high sensitivity for the art, a passion for cooking, and the enjoyment of music.

Gorman understood that if the creative process became infuriating after hours of work, it would be a fatal flaw to the final arrangement on the canvas. He knew that taking occasional breaks from painting improves creativity and productivity. Cooking was another way of expressing himself, away from colors and lines. Music was his relaxation.

Virgina Dooley, a graduate from the College Conservatory of Cincinnati with a major in voice and a minor in piano, was working as a music teacher in Taos. To supplement her music salary, she was selling lunches to the local businesses. With Virginia, Gorman hit the trifecta: she was a music teacher, loved art, and was an excellent cook.

She started by helping part time in the gallery on weekends and eventually, she became the full time gallery's director.

The other important woman in Gorman's life was his housekeeper and cook Rose Roybal.

These two women relieved Gorman of the responsibilities that weren't priorities for him. For instance, running the gallery, scheduling events, bookkeeping, promoting his art, taking care his home and cooking for him. They did whatever was necessary to prevent him from getting distracted from his art. Virginia, Rose and Gorman, besides their bonding friendship, made a dynamic team that propelled R.C. Gorman to new heights. In addition to the sharing of mutual interests in food, art and music, the trio loved to throw a party. After a hard day's work, the evenings in the gallery became a joyful space for good food, wine, celebrating with friends, having weddings, birthdays, and even wakes. They also organized events outside of the gallery and at times for noble causes.

Throughout history, female artists have been overlooked for their artistic ability. There were only a few women that emerge from obscurity and imposed themselves into the male-dominated art society. It wasn't until the social, political, and cultural movements in the sixties when female artist emerged to open new frontiers in the art landscape.

Even though female artists continually faced challenges due to gender biases in the art world, the movement was too powerful to stop women expressing their feelings on the canvas.

Gorman's team, keeping up with their innovating concepts, was active in promoting art by women. They organized the first all women artist exhibition in 1972 in Taos. The event was promoted heavily by Gorman himself and was an enormous success.

Gorman also insisted that his team make it a priority to help new upcoming artists and he took time from his usual heavy schedule to promote new artists. This was the case with Dan Namingha, in 1973. Namingha, a Hopi artist, recently discharged from the Marines, did his first one-man exhibit in R.C. Gorman's gallery. The event was extremely successful, and after a couple more shows, Namingha exhibited permanently in a gallery in Scottsdale, Arizona. He later became an internationally known artist.

Ultimately, Virginia and Rose allowed R.C. Gorman to center his energy in his art.

11

FINDING R.C. GORMAN

"Who is Rudolph Carl Gorman?"

A passing glimpse into his life reveals an interesting person who lived an unconventional life.

But the profound answer for this idiosyncratic character is intriguingly complex.

"Which Gorman are we referring to?"

A child born into poverty.

A young man trying to survive in a prejudiced society.

A struggling artist who, against insurmountable odds, separated himself from the pack. A creator of one-of-a-kind art to inspire generations of artists.

A benevolent visionary or the one who, at the end, sank into wealth and alcohol.

Enduring thousands of hours of research about a person that I have never met, I came to believe that he carefully cultivated his bigger-than-life persona.

While it is a true expression that he enjoyed the journey of his success by celebrating life to the fullest, it reveals only one side of the man; a fraction of what he feels and thinks.

Perhaps the good times were a reward for dealing with the challenging times; the extent of joyfulness responsible for the beauty of his work and its vast popularity.

"Who is R.C. Gorman?"

He is a Native American who wanted to live the American Dream. The poor kid from the reservation who wanted a better life, to supersede the temporary darkness with the bright lights.

He succeeded, in fact, he did it in a white man's world. He did it with unwavering determination, consistent vision and of course, his immense talent.

Nevertheless, as a newborn child, he wasn't expected to leave the hospital alive. The world would not know about R.C. Gorman if wasn't for the unusual nourishment of his great grandmother that kept him alive.

To uncover Gorman's inner world, I had to search for some of his unique earlier paintings, those created on moments of melancholy and romanticism. Moments when the images on the canvas captured his realistic, raw emotions.

The Enigma Suite was one of those moments.

For a while, I stood at the crossroads, perplexed about his reasoning and ability to choose the direction he has taken by powering his way to prominence. Obviously, the path he took was to the right direction, but many questions remained answered.

How did Gorman surface from obscurity?

Out of the thousands talented artists, why him?

Was he true to his art until the end?

For an artist, crossing the bridge to prosperity is a dangerous path, a double edge sword. First, one must adjust his attitude, to grow, to leave behind the Bohemian mindset of the "starving artist." Then, when he gets there, he must endure the intoxication of success and remember that what brought him there was the love of his art.

It is a challenging undertaking for a celebrity to maintain modesty, to somehow endure the bright lights of fame.

At this point of my narrative, R.C. Gorman is on that bridge, crossing on towards the stage of fame and wealth. I am standing right along with him – trying to understand what is waiting on the far side.

In front of me lies the tormenting blank page that mocks me, the anguish of the elusive sentence and the evasive completed page. I am looking back.

What have I missed?

Eventually, I discover some forgotten art that might define a portion of his beliefs and sensitivities; virtues that should help to test his trueness while across that bridge.

To understand some of the symbolism of Gorman's rare pieces, first, we must understand the Navajo culture, their celebrations, rituals, and traditions.

Many traditional Navajo supernatural powers are given human images; others viewed as various animals or natural phenomena. The Navajo deities are dominant in the Navajo daily life, especially in their many holiday dances, art displays and folktales. Their songs are mostly prayers to supernatural beings, asking for blessings for a healthy and happy life, curing the sick, or protecting their animals and the harvest.

The Navajo creation story is an evolution of several underworlds. At the beginning, it was the dark world, surrounded by four clouds. White on the east for the dawn, yellow for twilight on the west, blue for daylight on the south and black for the night on the north. The Navajo deities and heroes climbed out from the dark world and onto several layers of different worlds. They survived the darkness and destruction of these underworlds to finally surface to live in the white world, to give the Navajo people the necessary knowledge to survive and to protect Mother Earth.

Monster Slayer and *Born for Water* were the twin offspring of *Sun* and *Changing Woman*. The twins came to the white world to protect the people from monsters and to help them live in harmony. Along their journey the twins met the small but mighty *Spider Woman*.

One of the most important deities of traditional Navajo religion is *Spider Woman*. She is always helping those in need, protects the innocent, and restores harmony in the universe.

R.C. Gorman's Homage to *Spider Woman* show at The Smithsonian's National Museum of the American Indian Art featured several rare drawings and lithographs and disclosed some of Gorman's inner feelings and the respect for his culture.

Gorman's earlier work demonstrated his eloquent drawing ability and reveals his sensitive approach to the human form. His lesser-known explorations of Navajo textile designs are a tribute to *Spider Woman,* who taught the Navajo women how to weave.

Gorman's *Spider Woman* painting is a testament to his power to portrait vivid expressions with seemingly simple strokes of his brush. Gorman claimed that she gives him knowledge, she tells him what to do.

In his *Spider Woman* painting, the focal point is the bottom part of the image where the creases of her dress fold into a spider web and her left hand is pushing the ground, ready to spring into action. Her face is determined and fearless, daring anyone to test her strength. If I had to guess the next words coming out of her mouth it would be, "dare me," or to evoke De Niro's signature facial expression of toughness saying, "You talking to me?"

Gorman's four-color lithographic print titled *"Yei-bi-chai"* is a tribute to the sacred Navajo celebration.

The purpose of the celebration is to maintain the harmony between the people and the universe. It is spearheaded by the Medicine Man and goes on for nine days.

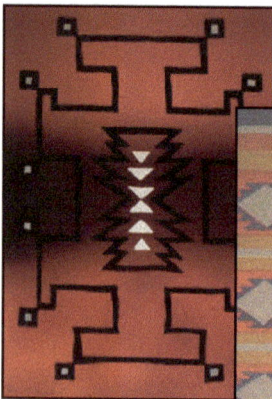

Spider Woman
I

Spider Woman
II

Spider Woman
III

Spider Woman
IV

Yei-bi-chai

Spider Woman

To the Navajo people, harmony is equivalent to health and beauty and any disturbance of harmony causes emotional, physical illness and spiritual injury. This ceremony is usually held during the coldest time of the year. If possible, they try to avoid natural disruption, like lightning, thundering or rain. It is also the time when the snakes are hibernating. To the Navajo snakes are a sign of poisonous threat to the people and their livestock. Thunder and lightning are reminiscent of the dark world and they believe that sickness, health, and death are dependent on the mood and the will of the power behind these elements. The primary colors and symbols of their ancestors are permanent during the ceremony, in blue and white masks, yellow, white, and red clothing along with eagle feathers.

To the Navajo, the color blue represents peace and happiness. The mountain bluebird is associated with the rising sun and is a symbol of life. The ceremony ends with the chanting of the *Bluebird Song*.

Gorman's *Night Stories* is most likely another tribute to his beloved *Spider Woman* who, according to the legend, also rescued and disciplined Navajo boys. Symbolically, this is a dominant piece, and most likely one of Gorman's most valuable paintings. Aside from the impressive aesthetics of the painting, Gorman illustrates several significant messages here. The painting shows a little boy standing by his mother, seeking knowledge about the universe. They both stand at the edge of the Navajo sacred mountain; he is pointing to five symbols on the star-dotted blue sky. Aligned on top of the sky is the dog, which symbolized the healing of emotional wounds and unquestioned loyalty. Behind it is the rabbit, a symbol of fear and overcoming limiting beliefs. Next is the sheep, the backbone of survival and centering of the human energy in the universe. Right behind it is the deer, a sign of patience, considering irreversible decisions carefully and to protecting the family. Below, guarding them is the alligator, a symbol of stealth and the fight for survival.

Night Stories

During my quest to find whatever useful information about Gorman I met individuals who knew him well and others who pretended to know him. Some of those who knew him well expressed various opinions about R.C. Gorman; some were cordial, others bias or envious. Those who knew him by reputation or by a quick interaction shrugged their shoulders; some smiled politely, and a few went on to criticize relying on baseless information.

The bottom line is that nobody knows an individual completely other than himself. Gorman's life companions, the two women, knew him well in the later part of his life. Friends and family, simply knew a big part of him. The rest of us simply know his public life.

R.C. Gorman was not immune to feelings and emotions, like none of us are, but, we all have certain talents, secrets, insecurities, weakness, and strengths. I have long given up my search for the perfect human being - perfection is a beast trapped within us.

Remember the couple that walked in the Scottsdale gallery?

You know, the wife who either loved Gorman's works or she pretended to like the art, just to be hip.

What about the husband, did he not like Gorman's work or he stood his ground to just "be the man." We will forever speculate.

Some time ago, before I even thought about researching and writing about the Navajo spiritual world, I met a gentleman at a grocery check-out line of all places. It was in one of my visits to Taos.

He was a middle-aged gentleman, standing in front of me, ready to pay for something he had packaged in a nice brown box.

What intrigued me was the question he asked the checkout lady, "The product in this box is eighty-nine cents per pound. Do I have to pay for the weight of the box?"

"That is an interesting question," I instantly responded. It is something that I would have never thought of.

We started a conversation and the two of us ended up sitting at the grocery's coffee shop for the next couple of hours.

When I told him about what I was doing, he responded with, "I love Gorman's work. I have some of his earlier paintings."

Well, what do you know!

He continued, "I am an art collector. It is the reason I come to Taos. The pieces of Gorman's work I have are originals, produced in the late seventies. I am conflicted about selling or keeping them."

"If you like his art, why sell it?"

He paused for a moment. "In my opinion, he did not use his artistic ability and position to achieve a deeper recognition in the more serious part of the art community."

I was surprised to hear his view. I decided not to react and let his opinion simmer a bit in my head. He was well dressed, most likely in his early sixties, well-spoken and carried himself with authority. If I had to guess, he was either a lawyer or a politician.

"Interesting." I managed to say

"Where is your accent from?"

"Greek."

Most people who learn about my heritage talk about the islands, food, weather, Zorba, the Three Hundred, the Big Fat Greek Wedding, miss-pronounce Gyros, Leonidas, my name; but this gentleman, based on his next question, seemed to know his history.

"Do you like the stoic or the cynic philosophy?"

A confrontational approach to a conversation! I thought. Like asking someone on the first meeting bold questions about status and ideology; Republican or Democrat. Religious or Godless. Rich or Poor.

But okay. I am game. "The Stoics of course."

He wasted no time. "It is too bad the Europeans have abandoned stoicism."

A curious perspective, I thought. A statement that was encompassing an entire continent under one theorization. I wanted to say that humanity has always found its way to the light, but I wasn't there to talk about the evolution of human behavior. All I wanted was some information about Gorman. "You know, Gorman loved to read philosophy," I said.

But he was relentless. "Yes, yes, Seneca was the last martyr of stoicism."

I wanted to avoid the subject, but I could not help myself.

"Why do you think Seneca was a martyr?"

"Well, he died for his beliefs. The way Socrates did."

"I do not see the similarity. Socrates took his life willingly, unlike Seneca who was ordered by Nero to take his life because he, supposedly, was involved in a plot to kill Nero."

"Nevertheless, it was the last heroic act of Stoicism."

"No one denies his contribution, but the last of the Stoics? What about Emperor Marcus Aurelius, who sought to rule justly according to the principle of Stoicism, and Hypatia over three-hundred years later who was killed by a mob of Christians while a fire burned the Library of Alexandria, destroying her important work?"

"Since we are on the subject of Gorman, I am comparing the Europeans with some of the Native American tribes. Especially the Navajo and Hopi people. I believe that when you try to balance the shifting between the old and new world; you find an unstable transition. However, I was impressed when I visited the villages of native people, it allowed me to observe their intensity. Their dance movements reflected the passion of long ago. Their eyes were filled with a special fire, something that I have not noticed with Europeans." He said calmly, as he slowly kept eating the sweets out of that brown box. He offered me some; I shook my head in refusal.

I was not sure the point that he wanted to make, although I partially disagreed, I did not want to prolong the subject.

Today we portray the Stoics as people with stern expressions and solemn hearts, who suppress their feelings. But, throughout the centuries, the Stoics cared about the human soul. The most dreadful thing for the Stoics is to lose control of the soul, to be confused in an egoistic struggle to find happiness in the outside world, over things which were not of their own power.

Socrates kindled the burning flame of Stoicism and Zeno defined it much later, using four of Socrates' chief virtues, Wisdom, Courage, Temperance, and Justice. These virtues have been used by many scholars throughout history as a teaching paradigm.

Through the passing of time, the Stoics have modified their message which has now become; to live in agreement with nature. It is against the Stoics beliefs to take pleasure in irrational elations. For instance, rejoicing at another's misfortunes, to be captivated by materialism, to be envious of desire and to give in to distress and fear, especially the fear of death. In a way, I agreed with this stranger who was chain-eating sweets while talking about health and beauty. A man who worries paying for the weight of a few ounces of a box while he is about to give away paintings worth a fortune.

I was at odds with his definition of Seneca's suffering to martyrdom. I believe that those who lost their life's work suffered the most, like the great Cicero whose library was torched; a crime against humanity. As far as impact throughout the ages, Cicero defined stoic oratory. He so eloquently combined the written word with the spoken one; a mixture of Demosthenes and Plato in one package. He paved the way for the great orators of today to evoke passion and substance in their speech. It is unfortunate that most of the orators of today are giving us speeches friendly to the ear but damaging to the soul. Most of their speeches do not inspire to improve the social makeup. The poor and the rulers are not in harmony with the middle class as they should be in a truly democratic society.

I wanted to tell my new friend that there was so much more beyond Seneca, all the way up to Descartes, whose great contribution was to tell us that ethics was a science, that like the rest of the sciences, ethics had its roots in philosophy. And yes, there is an amazing resemblance of stoicism in the Navajo beliefs about the elements that cause emotional and physical illness.

The Navajo snakes, to the Stoics, are the vicious people. The disturbance of thunder and lightning are equivalent to the Stoics averting distress and fear.

As my companion kept on talking, I had to find a polite way to break off this meeting. The subject was taking a labyrinthine twist. At this point, I wanted to go. I was tired from the long drive from Scottsdale.

"Why not keep it?" I asked

"Keep what?" he responded with a surprised tone as if he had forgotten the origin of this conversation

"Your Gorman pieces."

"Oh, that. I believe it would be best in a Museum. What do you think?"

"I am not sure what to tell you. It is your choice to make."

He scrolled through some of Gorman's paintings on his phone, as if he was trying to decide. "Look at these earlier pieces. It should be available for a public view." He said as he pointed the screen at me.

I remembered the piece called *Night Stories* and asked him to find it. He glanced at it for a while and pointed out the reflection of the fire at the bottom corner of the image.

"This painting shows the reflected glow of a ritual fire in the night time of the *Mountain Chant,* ceremony, held for healing. This one belongs in a Museum as well."

I had not noticed the reflection until he mentioned it. He was right.

Fire symbolizes the heart of the people and its smoke is used to cleanse sacred items before ceremonial use. Fire and its smoke carry prayers to the Great Spirit. The Fire represents cleansing and renewal because out of the ashes of fire comes new growth and new thoughts and ideas.

"I believe the *Night Stories* piece was created by R.C. Gorman in the mid-nineties. It is one of his latest pieces." I pointed out.

I wanted to make a point about his theory of Gorman abandoning his beliefs. He pressed his lips, shook his head and said nothing.

Night had fallen.

I walked away without knowing his name but knowing that he liked sweets – a lot of them. I've also learned that he did not have to pay for the box in the grocery store – the scale subtracts the weight of the box. This conversation inspired me to look deeper into Navajo spiritual world and now, maybe, I was ready to go onto his journey beyond the bridge. But first, if R.C. wanted to go places, he had to learn how to drive.

12

THE SAN FRANCISCO PACK

Occasionally, in order to understand Gorman's character, I look back into his childhood to find an example of an event that might have affected Gorman's reasoning.

One of these occasions was when he was still Rudy in grade school. He had worked tirelessly for a few days to make a clay molding for the school's art show. When done, the clay had been formed into a Mexican man resting under a saguaro cactus with his sombrero pulled over his face. Rudy was so excited about his clay model that he could hardly sleep that night. The next morning, anxious to go to school, he even skipped his breakfast. But, when he got to school, he was confused and heartbroken; his clay model was destroyed, broken into little pieces.

Who would to such a thing? Who would destroy art?

A few days later, at the school's art show, one of the school bullies presented a clay molded figure just like Rudy's. The bully was praised for his work. Rudy was furious. He was also determined to make a clay model better than the last one, one that no one would be able to copy. This traumatic experience taught Rudy that copying someone's art is theft.

R.C. always struggled with titles for his pieces since, for him, titles were the most difficult things to come by. For instance, he did not have a name for his relaxing Mexican man.

R.C. always maintained his great respect for the masters of the art and as well that of his contemporaries. He believed that to copy, especially a struggling contemporary, is like kidnapping someone's child - to copy a master is sacrilegious.

Ironically, later in his life, when people were copying his art, he felt that an artist isn't great until he is copied.

The other event that left its footsteps in Gorman's mind was much later when he was a young artist in San Francisco.

In the early nineteen-hundreds, the world was entering a new and unique age.

This exciting moment of time truly led artists to believe that they were part of a new visual expression for the modern world and they began to envision new ideas of what art should be. Often, the artist's attitude was radicalized by historical events and of political affiliation. The various revolts around the world for human dignity changed the mood and motivation of the arts.

The Great Depression in the United States diminished the purchasing ability of many art lovers. However, some artists, growing up during those challenging times found their path to fame. Many of those artists who became famous never lost their romanticism for their art. As they aged, they used their celebrity status to discover and support new talented artists. In their effort to introduce new artists to the world, they accompanied wealthy collectors, encouraging them to buy art from the struggling artists and help them out of obscurity.

In the early sixties, it was the trendy thing to do.

Tamara de Lempicka, one of the first women artists to be a glamorous star, was one of those helping artists. Her distinctive and fearless artistic style best represented the refreshing yet sensual part of the Art Deco movement. Known as Baroness Tamara de Lempicka Kuffner, a title earned by her latest marriage to Baron Raoul Kuffner, she lived a long and adventures life. During one of the greatest decades in art, the twenties in Paris, the so-called *Roaring Twenties of Paris*, she was part of the unconventional artist's life there, hanging out, with Picasso, Gide, Dali, and Cocteau.

In the early thirties, she traveled to Chicago to work with Georgia O'Keeffe and Willem de Kooning. In the late thirties, she spent most of her time painting around Hollywood stars, who referred to her as *The Baroness With a Brush.*

Lempicka, earlier in her career, became the center of intense criticism, as well as a great admiration, for her work, *Group of Four Nudes.* She retired from an active professional art career in the early sixties. This was the time she began her visits to R.C. Gorman's studio.

It was a springtime afternoon; a light rain had just washed out the thickness of the air, showing a delightful sun over the great city on the bay. It was the perfect afternoon for ladies to stroll the hilly streets of the city.

Gorman could not enjoy that glorious afternoon, he was working in his studio, in the lightless basement of the huge gray building. It was the only place he could afford to stay at the time.

There was a knock on the door. Standing outside was Baroness Tamara de Kuffner, along with two other ladies in their springtime elegant dresses and hats. It was Tamara's second visit to Gorman's studio. He offered the ladies coffee and water, the only things he had in his apartment. Obviously the ladies did not mind, they were expecting the bohemian treatment.

After a lengthy gossip about other artists, the ladies examined Gorman's work. As they were talking, Gorman was fascinated with Tamara's deep sexy voice and asked her to teach him how to roll his tongue. After spending some time mastering his rolling R's, Tamara said that she especially loved his *Black Matador.* The ladies bought some of his art and asked Gorman to bring it to the Regency Hotel where they were staying so they would have a chance to hang out with him again. For Gorman, this was a memorable encounter with one of the most glamorous female stars of the art community.

Even though, San Francisco, during the sixties, was the epicenter of nondiscrimination. The question, "What is an Indian doing in the white man's world?" occasionally surfaced in Gorman's mind. But then, he would meet up with his friends and all his doubts would go away. To his friends, he was just Gorman.

At first, there was Donna. She was a teacher and looked the part. She had dark hair, her glasses made her look smart and she dressed conservatively. She invited Gorman to her house often. This is where he met Lia, who was the antithesis of Donna. She usually wore men's jeans, a gray sweatshirt and tennis shoes. She, unlike Donna, was heavy set and short with washed blond hair. They both invited Gorman into their homes, feeling sorry that he was alone. And then there was Clint, his wife Darlene, Bob, Raymond, and Mary Beth. These friends slowly formed a San Francisco pack.

At this time Gorman had not completely thrown himself into his art. He was working various part-time jobs and hanging out with his friends.

Some nights he loved to cook. He would have everyone pitch in to buy the ingredients and then he would make affordable dinners for his friends. His favorite meal to make was spaghetti with tomato sauce. He believed that blending herbs to bring out a great taste is the highest of arts.

How could anybody resist the smell of garlic and onions sautéed in olive oil and blended with fresh tomatoes? That coupled with a good salad, some famous San Francisco sourdough bread and wine, made a memorable dinner.

Some days, he and his friends would gather up some money, go to the airport, and order a couple of glasses of beer. They would sip the beer and watch the jets takeoff and land. They were dreaming of places to go, looking at posters of Spain, Italy, Greece or Argentina and imagining beautiful places, unique foods and exotic drinks.

Clint and Lia were Gorman's closest friends. Clint gave him rides to work since Gorman didn't drive.

In those years Gorman moved often, mostly because he could not afford rent.

Moving around was no problem, most of his belongings were his painting gear and his friends were there to help him move.

Clint and Bob sometimes helped Gorman with his art. They learned how to stretch canvas and make crates, and even found models for Gorman.

Raymond was an athlete, a long-distance runner.

The gathering of friends continued, no matter how small their living quarters. There was music, long talks, drinking painting, reading, and of course there was home cooked food. The friends were mostly students and artists, working low paying jobs. They occasionally went to the movies. Gorman stayed home when it was a western movie – he did not want to see his people being portrayed as clueless Indians.

As the years went by, Lia gradually started to change, she left her strange look behind, lost a lot of weight and looked great.

One year Gorman had a Christmas party in his place. There were over two hundred people who came to celebrate. Everyone was invited, the landlord, lawyers, the dentist, a stripper, the clerk from the grocery story. Everyone, including a psychiatrist with whom Lia fell in love. A rich friend, Scott donated many gallons of dry wine, and a lot of people brought liqueur and beer, and snacks.

The party was in the basement on Castro Street. The place was very small. It was amazing that all these people had room to move around, drink and dance.

Everyone had a great time and talked about that party for the weeks to come.

However, shortly after the party there was a tragedy.

Clint wanted Gorman to make a little design for his mother's birthday. It was past their one o'clock meeting time. Gorman was worried and called his house. Darlene answered, her voice breaking, she told Gorman that Clint died earlier this morning.

Gorman was shocked.

It was just yesterday when a group of friends, including Clint, went across the bay to visit the Oakland arts and crafts. Now he is dead!

She told him that "Clint came home late last night after a concert; he was feeling warm. So, he tried to open a window that was stuck. It was one of those sash windows that you have to push up. In his effort to open it, Clint fell out of the window and died."

Gorman became depressed - Damn you, Clint, people don't fall out of the windows and die!

A month later Lia's brother died. He killed himself.

By now the group was drifting apart; people were moving away, people were dying, people were starting families.

Eventually, Donna moved to Greece, Darlene to Japan, with her father who was in the Navy, and Mary Beth to Mexico

To deal with the ongoing changes in the streets of San Francisco, Gorman went to Mexico for the first time, a trip that was a turning point in his life. In Mexico, he reconnected with Mary Beth, who had modeled for him.

During the next few years, Gorman kept in touch with his friends.

Lia was having a tough time with her brother's loss.

Darlene was writing from Japan, still devastated by Clint's loss.

Gorman went back to San Francisco, his art started selling well. He could afford a nicer place, the one on the top of the hill, on Army Street.

Lia moved to Wyoming. She got pregnant and wanted to have the child and give it for adoption.

Phil, an old schoolmate, never stopped loving Lia. He moved to Wyoming and proposed to marry her and take care the baby. She was skeptical at first, but Phil has finally succeeded in persuading her to marry him.

Phil treated Lia like a queen and loved Kathy, her baby, like his own.

While in San Francisco, Gorman received a letter from an art dealer, Mr. Helder. He had seen Gorman's work in Scottsdale and was excited to handle some of Gorman's art. After Gorman sent him a fairly large amount of his work, Helder told him that it was not what he expected. He said that he did not want the pastels, which was what he had requested initially. He said he now wants watercolors. From all the work Gorman did, he ended up buying only two pieces and sent Gorman forty dollars. What is a man supposed to do with forty dollars? – It hardly covered the expenses for the materials, never mind his time. Of course, this greedy dealer was going to make huge profits. He then had the audacity to ask for more art.

Helder was going to ship the rest of the art to other dealers to sell. Gorman responded, saying that the forty dollars was not enough, he wanted more for his work.

The trading post experience, stealing his art, and this dealer, doubled Gorman's certainty that most art dealers were not to be trusted. It seemed to him that they were put on this earth to take advantage of artists. They made him feel like they were doing him a favor. Unlike collectors, who bought art for the love of it. He often thought, "When I become famous, you will come to me".

Then there was another bad day. The director of the Philbrook Art Center wrote saying that only his oil paintings were accepted for his second exhibition which was scheduled with his dad. The director loved them, but the jury team did not accept them as they considered it graphic work – it is art guys!

But, soon there was a marvelous surprise, The Heard Museum in Phoenix, bought one of his large oil paintings. And then, the Jewish community center in Tucson, bought two more of his paintings.

After the many years of pinching pennies to survive, Gorman finally felt rich.

But, the struggles continued and the doubts kept surfacing. There was no looking back, Gorman had to push forward and endure the storms.

Emotional memories are infinite, frozen in time, into the safest chambers of our subconscious mind and surface in a time of doubt and concern. Like his memory in grandmother's place when the summer heat vanished into the cool night breeze off the Waterless Mountain and grandmother would name all the stars for Rudy. Or, when he played with his cousins in the Chinle Wash as the rains were pouring down, body surfing, voices of joy filling the air, their little bodies pushed onto the side, into the mud, and back to the water.

And so also the memory of the art dealers taking advantage of him never left him.

Gorman bought a parrot. He used to tell people that wasn't a true parrot because it never talked, until one day the parrot said, "Hello" when Gorman was looking at him. After that he had taught his parrot to say some nasty words whenever an art dealer visited him.

13

DEAR MOTHER

During my research on R.C. Gorman I noticed that he seldom mentions his mother. I was curious, so I went back to his childhood.

Rudy was the oldest child. Carl Gorman, his father, said his good-byes and enlisted at Fort Defiance, on his way to serve the armed forces of the United States. Fort Defiance is near the town of Widow Rock, in the southeast borders of Arizona and New Mexico. But, for his children, Rudy, Don and Donna, it seemed like it was at the end of the world.

Fort Defiance was established in 1851 to create a military presence in the Navajo Land. It was built on valuable grazing land, considered holy for the Navajo people. As its name suggests, Fort Defiance had a turbulent past. For the decade after establishment, the Navajo fought to reclaim their land. The fighting escalated, especially when the federal government prohibited the Navajo to use the land. The defiant Navajo warriors continued their raids, even knowing that they were outnumbered. Finally, the much superior U.S. Army prevailed. At this time, thousands of starving Navajos were taken out of their land and forced into the historic four hundred and fifty mile *Long Walk* to the Bosque Redondo concentration camp.

Today the concentration camp is a monument to pay homage to the Navajo struggles. Carl Gorman and a group of Navajo code talkers reported to Ford Defiance, and from there were taken for basic training to the San Diego Marine Corps Recruit Depot.

Some of the members of the group were underage, but as birth records were not usually kept on the reservation, a recruit could claim any age. Carl Gorman's problem was that at thirty-six years old, he was too old to be considered by the Marines, so he lied about his age to be accepted.

Rudy and his siblings felt proud, but sad that their dad was going to serve their country. Rudy noticed that his mother, Adele, did not seem proud or sad. There was certainly a rift between his mother and father. Springtime was fading away in the reservation. The first windy days were forecasted followed by rainy days and snow falling. Adele packed their few belongings and told the children that they were moving. She told the children that she was offered a job outside Flagstaff.

"Mother, this place it is not on the reservation," Rudy thought.

Adele, among many other Navajos, was given a job in the Ordinance Depot in Bellemont, a place just west of Flagstaff. It was a place used for the storage of ammunition during World War II, and one of the largest storage bases in the country.

The children had no choice. They left the only house the have ever known, their school, their friends and did as their mother told them. Rudy's father expected him to be the family leader; he had the responsibility to reassure his younger siblings that they would be safe in the outside world. Maybe there was a better school and better food there?

The army piled the Gorman family along with other Navajos into covered troop trucks and hauled them away. Everyone huddle together, uncertain what was beyond. After riding for a while, the trucks stopped in Hopi Indian land, which sat in the middle of the Navajo land.

The children had never been so far away from home and the excitement made them tremble. They embraced one another.

Everyone was herded into a trading post. Rudy explained to his brother and sister that the trading post is a store where Indians bring goods and crafts to trade for groceries and supplies. The traders would then sell the goods and crafts to dealers off the reservation, make a profit, and bring back more groceries. Rudy had been in a trading post before - but in this one had something new and exciting for sale: oil paintings.

The beautiful paintings memorized Rudy.

Even the Catholic Church which had pretty windows, candlesticks and images of saints had nothing like these paintings.

"How could something like this exist?"

"Rudy, let's go." mother insisted. "They aren't going to wait around for us."

"How could anyone make such beautiful pictures of the canyons and the sky?"

"The truck is leaving." mother shouted.

"What did they use?" More than anything, Rudy wanted to learn how to do this.

His mother's hand pulled him away.

As they rode towards Flagstaff, Rudy wondered about the Indian artist who made those pictures?

Their truck came to a stop. People got off the trucks and were taken to the barracks. The camp was enclosed with wire fences.

There was a tremendous activity as people were searching for their living quarters, soldiers scrambling to help, children crying. This seemed like a tough place to live.

Rudy remembered herding the sheep and goats into fenced corrals in the reservation. But, here it was the people herded around the fenced land. Their mother tried to explain this was a place protecting the ammunition to fight bad people with. But Rudy wasn't listening. He couldn't stand this feeling, of being fenced. He wanted to run free.

"Mother, this is not a place to raise children."

The barracks were cold and the crude toilets and showers were outdoors and shared with everybody else. A bus arrived every day to take the Native American children to public school in Flagstaff. The family tried to keep up with their father's whereabouts. Nobody knew where he and the other Navajo men were. All they knew was that the men were on a secret mission.

Shortly after they arrived in the camp, a strange thing happened, high wired fences were built around them and soon afterwards, truckloads of foreign white men arrived. They spoke a strange language. Rudy learned that they were German prisoners.

"Was America now fighting Germany?"

Adele and her children lived with the Germans on their side. It was the winter of 1943.

Rudy was restless, dreaming about those paintings in the trading post. His mother was too busy to discipline the children and she began spending a lot of time with another man. She seemed to be getting along better with this man than she did with his dad.

"I know what you are doing, mother."

Rudy wasn't happy about this. His dad was his hero and the thought that he will be heartbroken upon his return was upsetting. His mother reminded Rudy about the priests and nuns back at the church when he was an altar boy.

"Alter boy? I hated it, but I am listening."

There was a school like that, called Saint Michaels near Gallup, New Mexico. They take care of Native American children. His mother had made arrangements for Rudy to live there.

"You are twelve now they will take you." his mother said.

"Are you trying to get rid of me, mother?"

Rudy asked her when was his father coming home and if he would come to see him in that school. "Of course, he will come," his mother said, "but you must understand that things will never be the same again for our family."

What Rudy didn't know was that once he went to that school near Gallup, he too would not be the same again.

He yearned for his dad. He looked out the window often, anticipating seeing him walking home. He disliked what his mother was doing; his father was fighting for his country and his mother abandoned him, and now she was sending Rudy away.

"What about the other children?"

The Saint Michael Mission school was not a pleasant experience for Rudy.

Besides speaking only English, the nuns cut his hair, wanted him to change his name and he was not learning anything of interest. He was constantly hungry.

He had never been this hungry before in the reservation there was always food. Family and friends would make sure there were groceries or they would butcher a sheep or be invited to various ceremonial parties.

The days were frigid and the clothing light. He was never so cold in his life as when they marched to mass or to class.

Boys and girls were separated. On his one day off, he was forced to shovel coal.

"This is not a school. This is a prison."

He yearned for food and some crayons to paint. He asked one of his friends if it was possible to get some crayons to draw. Rudy told him that in the public school in Chinle, he once drew a girl without her clothes on.

The friend responded by saying, "Don't do that here they will hang you on the cross."

They both had a good laugh.

This is the school he eventually was expelled from and hitchhiked back to the reservation.

There he stayed with his aunt Mary until, weeks later, his mother came to the reservation. She did not know what to do with him.

Rudy insisted that he would not go to any school that did not allow art - never again. His aunt suggested the Ganado Presbyterian Mission. Rudy agreed to go only if they allowed art. A few weeks later his mother came back, along with another man.

Rudy said, "I am not getting in the car with him."

After a bit of convincing, he gave a long hug to his aunt, thanked her for taking care of him, and got into the car. The man in the car tried to talk to Rudy.

"I am not talking to you."

The complex of Ganado Mission school was impressive and overwhelmed young Rudy. There were church dormitories, academic buildings, a hospital, a nursing school, barns and central power plants.

The place was an entire town.

Sadness overcame him. His father was gone for many years now, his mother was always working and now living with another man, and now she was abandoning him again.

A couple of boys welcomed him and greeted him in his own Navajo language. Rudy was pleasantly surprised that he could speak his language there. That was a positive start. The classes were in English but he was free to speak his language

He soon discovered that this was a wonderful place for him. It was a school that allowed him freedom, a comfortable living, good food, and most of all, encouraged the arts

One of his teachers gave him several books to read, some of them had beautiful illustrations made by Beaten Yazz, a Navajo boy. He was determined to learn how to do that.

The director of the school loved opera and drama and encourage the students to take piano lessons and try their compositions

The school raised all their livestock, produced their dairy products and grew fruits and vegetables. The students had to learn how to take care of a farm.

Rudy's favorite chore was to milk the cows early in the morning.

A petite woman Ms. Jenny Lind who volunteered a few days a week took an interest in Rudy's drawings. Ms. Lind guided Rudy into the library's books with pictures and drawings by Indian artists. Rudy told her that he wanted to draw like Beaten Yazz and Harrison Begay.

Ms. Lind gave him books from other artists around the world. From then on it was all about art. Soon Rudy was painting with oils, tempera, watercolor and drawing with pencil and ink

The years went by and with Ms. Lind's instructions Rudy produced large collections of charcoal drawings sketches and even some of oil and tempera paintings

At first, he drew the traditional way of other Indian artists with cartoon-like colorful forms, but his skills developed rapidly. At the end of his first year, Ms. Lind showed his collection to the staff of Ganado

Mission. All of Rudy's pieces sold for a couple of dollars each. He was now a working artist.

Rudy was thrilled. His dream was to take his work to a trading post where no one knew his name or age and see if it would sell.

Rudy was working on the grounds and farms of Ganado during summer breaks for tuition money and kept on reading and working on his art.

At the end of his first summer in Ganado, the war was over - Japan surrendered. He was immensely proud of his father and anxious to see him. He was distancing himself from his mother since he knew that he would not be living with her.

Rudy worked hard to improve his academics and art. One of the subjects he could not grasp well was math. He understood that football was also not for him, once he ran smack into a goalpost and knocked himself out.

The summer before his father's return, his young uncle Clarence, just a couple of years older than Rudy, told him that there was a good paying job in the Bright Angel Lodge, a hotel complex at the South Rim of the Grand Canyon. Rudy decided that it was time to make more money than what he was making working in the school, and followed his uncle to the Grand Canyon. They both worked as handymen in the lodge during the day, and bus boys in the evenings.

In their first few days off, Rudy was determined to find a trading post that accepted the art that he had been working on for the past year. He hitchhiked to Flagstaff, to get to Route 66, and kept hitchhiking east on 66 towards Gallup, where most of the trading posts were located. Once in the periphery of Gallup, he chose one of the trading posts and walked in carrying his best drawings in a folder. It was early afternoon and there were no customers in the post. The white woman running the post was polite and Rudy showed her his art. The lady told him that she would take his art as a consignment.

Rudy thanked her and left his paintings with her, saying that he would be back at the end of the summer. That was his first innocent transaction with business. In his excitement of someone willing to sell his work, he neglected to have any signed agreements, as was a customary practice with transactions in the trading posts.

Rudy found his way back to the Grand Canyon.

He and Clarence worked hard and had great fun helping the maids with heavy lifting items, scrubbing different areas, and painting walls and doors. They worked as bus boys in the Fred Harvey restaurant, which was part of the resort. They got to wear crisp white uniforms and tasted great foods.

Ms. Lind's books with the famous artists around the world, put another enticing thought in Rudy's head. He decided that someday he would travel to see those famous paintings and meet people of other cultures.

After an exciting summer in the Bright Angel Lodge, Rudy visited his mother who still lived and worked in Flagstaff. She was proud to see him earning money to cover his school expenses.

Before he went back to Ganado, Rudy eagerly hitched back to Gallup to find out if any of his paintings were sold at the trading post.

The white woman frowned when she saw the young boy walking in. Rudy noticed that all of his drawings were gone and asked how much money he made. "I don't know you boy, go away." was the woman's response.

"But my paintings are gone you must owe me money."

The woman turned and walked away saying that she did not know what drawings he was talking about. Rudy was furious but also helpless. The way back to the Grand Canyon was lonely and long.

"When I grow up, no dealer will steal my money again."

It was time to return to school. Upon his return, his teachers, especially Ms. Lind, welcomed him with smiles and kindness. This helped to restore his faith in the white people.

Later in life, he thought about his mother and how she always made sure there were clothes, food, and shelter for her children. He confessed that he would climb a mountain to light a candle for his mother.

"Dear mother, thank you."

14

CALL ME R.C.

Rudy graduated from Ganado in the class of 1950. He was near the top of his class, the author and star of the senior play and eager to take on the world.

His father returned from the war and the world was right again. Rudy went on to Flagstaff state college. But by now the wide world had opened its doors for Rudy, and he wanted to see as much of this world as possible.

Joining the Navy was one way to travel to different places. After his basic training at San Diego, he got his wish. For the next two years, he was stationed in the South Pacific.

Even though, during his young life, he had met a variety of people outside the reservation, the Navy gave him an opportunity to meet people of other cultures. Some of the airmen spoke slang with accents he had never heard before; they came from strange towns, from different religions, and unusual family backgrounds. Furthermore, most of these men were unfamiliar with Native Americans. At first, he was stationed at the naval base in Guam. This was a place much different that Gorman had imagined; a place of great beauty. There were lovely beaches, crystal clear water, deep green vegetation, and majestic sunsets.

While working for the Navy in Guam, he found time to take courses in English and journalism at Guam Territorial College, an extension of Ohio State University. Gorman's animated personality and the uniqueness of being the only Native American in the living quarters attracted attention. It was easy for him to make friends. His two shipmates Bryan Klages and Ron Rutt became his good friends.

After staying two years in Guam, R.C. went on to serve on the aircraft carrier USS Oriskany patrolling the pacific coast of the United States. He was discharged in 1955 and returned to Flagstaff college to study journalism. His family by now had scattered around. His father was working as an illustrator at Douglas Airport and was painting in Santa Monica. His mother had remarried and lived in the reservation raising several more children. His brother and sister were in their twenties and building their lives.

I located one of his buddies in the Navy, Bryan Klages, who is now living in Minnesota. I couldn't locate Ron Rutt, I believed he has passed away.

"Mr. Klages, tell me about R.C. Gorman?"

"I met R.C. in nineteen-fifty-three when I was in a watch in Guam," his voice animated, perhaps, remembering the days of youth.

He continued, "I saw a light in the bedding area and went to check it out. He was in there painting."

"Do you remember what the painting was?"

"Yes. I still remember it. It was a woman with a long red dress. He said it was his cousin. It was beautiful."

"Did you keep in touch with him after that?"

"We were in the same barracks, so I would talk to him after my watch. He was kind and very respectful to me. He listened to a lot of music, especially a Native American drum record he had recorded. He also enjoyed Eartha Kit's song "Santa Baby" plus some other songs of hers in foreign languages. Gorman said he couldn't understand them, but he was mesmerized by her voice."

I'm not sure what foreign songs Gorman was listening to, since Eartha Kit sang songs in a dozen different languages.

"Did you hang out with him, outside the base?"

"Well, yes, we had a few friends that used to go to the service club for drinks and to get supplies. I got out of the service in October of fifty-three."

"Did you ever hear from him again?"

"I was home for about a year when I got a letter from him and we kept in touch after that. My wife and I saw him when on vacation in Taos in the eighties. He had company, so we stayed in a hotel. He took us to dinner and paid our bill. He took me through his gallery and gave his art as gifts, for my wife and each of our six kids. He was very generous."

"Have you seen him again after that?"

"A few years later we went back to see him and we stayed as guests in his house. He showed us all around. We saw all his paintings, his swimming pool, garden. He had a big painting of his aunt who helped raise him. There were a lot of pictures of the mountains and famous people. He didn't say anything about his mother but talked about his dad. He joked that he thought he might have some half-brothers around some place. We stayed two nights in his guest house. One day he took us up to a resort which was closed, but the restaurant was open and he said they had great food. We drove about an hour up to the mountains to get there."

"What do you remember most about Gorman?"

"Once we got to know him well; the love in his heart. My wife still talks about R.C. He used to call my wife the jam lady because she often sent him a box of her homemade jam. I remembered when she made jams, she would put some jars away saying, 'Don't touch these, they are for R.C.' We also got Christmas cards from him every year."

He paused for a moment.

"When we learned of his death my wife was very sad."

"Is there a moment or two that sticks in your mind from the Navy days?" There was another short pause.

"He was always writing and painting. At first, we called him by his name, Rudolph. One day I walked up to him, called his name and asked him if he wanted to go to the service club."

He did not answer. After a moment he said, "Call me R.C."

"I guess I was the first one to call him R.C. From then on, everyone called him R.C."

Gorman explained later on that he never really liked the name Rudolph, and Rudy was a name for a child. He decided he needed a crisp name, to match his sharp white navy uniform.

R.C. Gorman is how he was introduced to the world.

15

COMING OF AGE

During his artistic evolution, the one thing that R.C. Gorman never changed was his use of the Navajo Madonnas. These had become his signature images.

Gorman's work, that he has done throughout his life, is predominately women. For Gorman, the female image was the vehicle for his statements about the human condition, sexuality, and aging.

Many young artists, during their growth, struggle to find their voices. It was no different for Gorman. However, going back as early as the mid-sixties, it is clear to see the emotions and expressions in his work, like in *Navajo Mother In Supplication*. His earlier work exhibit is a rich and complex mixture of emotional states.

Moving on to the decade of the seventies, we find more images around his women, like corn, flowers, birds and vases. His women are now more active, combing their hair, baking bread, climbing ladders, carrying baskets. He also added more colors to his paintings.

After that comes the series of nudes. Should this change of expression alarm concern? Nothing, in particular, was going on in Gorman's life at that time. I believe he just wanted to do something different. Maybe the temporary change in his artistic attitude was refreshing.

It seemed that the nudes were a cathartic experience for Gorman because soon after that, we noticed a signification emergence of his use of colors, as well as more influential mood expressions.

His works of rugs and masks were quite expressionistic, especially the red and orange colors. Most of his works, at this time, were lithographs, produced from acrylic paintings. The work that Gorman and his master printers were producing were losing very little in translation. They had mastered the art.

The emerging of colors was the first example of what was to be regarded next as emblematic Gorman. In his newest lithographs, his women's postures were changing; they were no longer alone and they were grouped together. The clothing of his women was expanding, and richer landscapes were showing up. New colors, new postures, adding new dresses and landscape, seems to be the stylistic bones from which Gorman would adopt in the future.

The impressive blend of colors and design in *Chief's Blanket* reflects Gorman's artistic brilliance. In both versions, the blanket is the focus point. In *Chief's Blanket I,* the red crosses against the red field, with the black lines against the white at the bottom, are an extraordinary visual feast of colors. In *Chief's Blanket II* the red and blue is a more soothing image.

In *Lighting Blanket,* another masterful and spellbound display of colors, the clothing is the primary subject. His women in these few pieces have gone from embodiment of strength to a simple character You can see, in these three pieces, that he is starting to identify the character of his women. In *Chief's Blanket,* the woman is obviously Oriental and in the *Lighting Blanket* she is Native American.

Chief's Blanket I

Chief's Blanket II

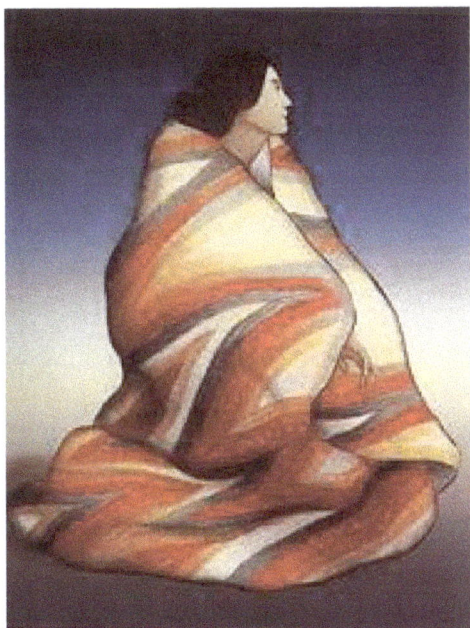

Lighting Blanket

In another change of pace, the woman in the *Woman with a Bowl,* is an older, white-haired woman, sitting with her back resting against a wall. I am not certain what is the meaning of her staring into an empty wooden brown bowl. I am sure Gorman had something in mind. But one thing is certain here – those omnipresent large brown feet were meant to be the focal point.

As we know, Gorman uses feet and hands as a symbolic imagery of the Native American's connection with the earth.

There is a flying woman in *Dream Night* and *Dream Day.*

This was a surprise to many. There were questions and concerns about this emerging image. The initial question from some of the loyal followers I spoke with was - What is wrong with Gorman? And the concern was – Is Gorman being influenced by all the science fiction movies that are starting to become popular?

Of course, this was not the case, but it is an interesting subject of discussion. The flying lady was not a Navajo superwoman and he was not getting into a superhero genre. Like the older couple I met in Santa Fe who were looking at that same image, after the initial shock, this image was justified as a calming imagery of death. The work was implemented in several stages as if the artist was searching for the right combination of image and message. The piece that makes a sincere statement about the vision of R.C. is the one with the royal blue sky, the flowing red robe, the faded stars and the mellow sunset over the desert. This woman is headed for heaven.

Dream Night

Woman with a Bowl

It was at this time that his lithographs were in full production. It proved to be the turning point of Gorman's legacy. The vast body of limited paintings and prints are one of the reasons that Gorman has achieved wide world fame. If he had limited his production to paintings and drawings, he would never have been able to produce the immense amount of work he left behind. His limited amount of work would have been purchased by a few art collectors.

To produce the best images of lithography, there must be the right chemistry between the artist and the master printer.

The process of painters developing their ideas is similar to writers, musicians or any artist who creates. When an artist starts a new painting, he is vaguely locked into an idea but when he starts it can unfold quickly. The printers then follow, like a musician in an orchestra, a quick reaction is essential to be in harmony, to execute and to advance their maestro's lead.

The involvement of the printing crew is to assist the performance of the mastermind of the symphony.

R.C. Gorman admitted that there was so much more that he did not know about the technical aspects of lithography. To understand your limitation is the first step to enlightenment, especially for an artist who must keep his or her creative mind thirsty for knowledge.

As Gorman gained more understanding about the technical aspect, and his printers began to grasp Gorman's ideas, and managed the distraction of his gregarious personality, the quality of the work produced was constantly improving.

The printers Gorman worked with, admitted that he was a perfectionist. He paid attention to every detail from start to finish. His energy was tireless. There was always classical music in the background. Yes, he talked and joked, and they all laughed, but when the time came to put on paper what he had conceived in his mind, the workplace was church-quiet. The only sound was the greased pencil moving on the surface of the stone.

Part of Gorman's perfectionist personality was to be a keen critic of his own work. Sometimes, just before starting the printing of an image created months ago, the colors had been selected and the printing staff ready, he would look and admit that the image wasn't ready for printing. Back to drawing board. He was not concerned about the work wasted or the money lost – it had to be right. He corrected the color and redefined the image, kept up his spirits and those around him by promising that the image, once done, would be more beautiful.

Once the corrections were made, there was the distinctive sound of the soft squishing, as the printers were running the large rubber rollers over ink. Then the silence as the printer transfers the folder to the paper, running the printing roller over the stone.

Lithography became more intense as he moved to the next decade. The dramatic increase in the colors used, made the process more complicated. Besides the evolution of colors, the drawings and figures has evolved as well.

The impressive changes were due to Gorman's evolution as an artist. His art style was influenced by his lifestyle, his endless travels, his constant reading and his fascination with the different cultures. These made him more sophisticated and, therefore, more complicated.

The evidence is his last work, the blockbuster images before his passing. They had become the most popular among his growing fan base.

The six pieces of the *Anniversary Suite* done in the late nineties, followed by *The Blue Gem, Gracias, Cassandra, Jubilee, Fatima, Tulip Tree.* Their sophisticated color arrangement along with detailed signature Gorman form, showed his artist mind in progression.

Watching the crowds flocking into R.C. Gorman's Navajo Galleries, I see people walking out with prints of *Mariposa, Navajo Velvet, Scarlet,* and the one with the spectacular curving line simplicity, *Proud Lady.* These and many more are works he did right before his passing.

But, to me, what stands out is his dramatic etching of his dad, done in 2002. A piece called *Dad,* is rarely seen anywhere. This piece reveals, the great love for his father and a different style approach. There is a vortex of lines and curves which shape his father's head. The long white hair and closed eyelids give an expression of a calming strength. The result is impressive.

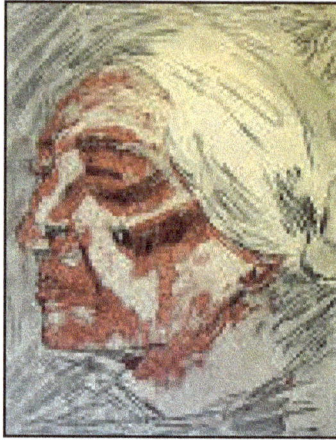

Dad

R.C. Gorman's artistic trials through six decades are symbolic of his endurance and success. His journey was like circling in a maze, searching for artistic freedom, on an ongoing path through narrow lines, corners, sharp edges and unknown destinations. At times, mundane and at times, immediate. His laser-like focus to find the exit of that maze, played a big part in urging him beyond the bending course.

His journey to fame would have never been possible if it wasn't for the immense demand for his art.

An unending circle starting from dealers that need the hottest art to sell, to art collectors, to the printers producing it, to the critics searching for newsworthy gossip. It went around and around. The artist is in the middle of it and without him, the circle ends. The true artist is concerned about his reputation, the quality of his work, but the unending circle demands, the different, the sexier and the refreshing. The work of the artist is affected, but the quality must never change or the circle would become a one-way street. The physiological pressure on the artist is overwhelming. How does one deal with this pressure? Isolation, alcohol, insanity, agitation? What? Somehow, some people do not believe in the theory of an unending circle but it is real. And those who live in it are caught in the whirlpool of infinite time. R.C. Gorman was caught in such a circle. As a young artist in San Francisco, he painted large realistic canvases of desert landscapes. Even back then he began to reveal his classical and rigid drawing style.

The progression of his work changed drastically from those simple and humble images. During transition periods, the artist can get temporarily lost until he defines his new vision. The important aspect of these gaps of transitions is not to weaken the urgency and spontaneity.

R.C. Gorman found himself in many crossroads during his long, enduring career. It seems that he chose the right direction. He broke new grounds, expanded his vision, and renewed his struggles. Like the song says, he did it his way.

And, talking about the unending circle of life, he ended up where he began; doing what he loved most in life – creating art.

Anniversary Suite - Madrid

Anniversary Suite - Delfina

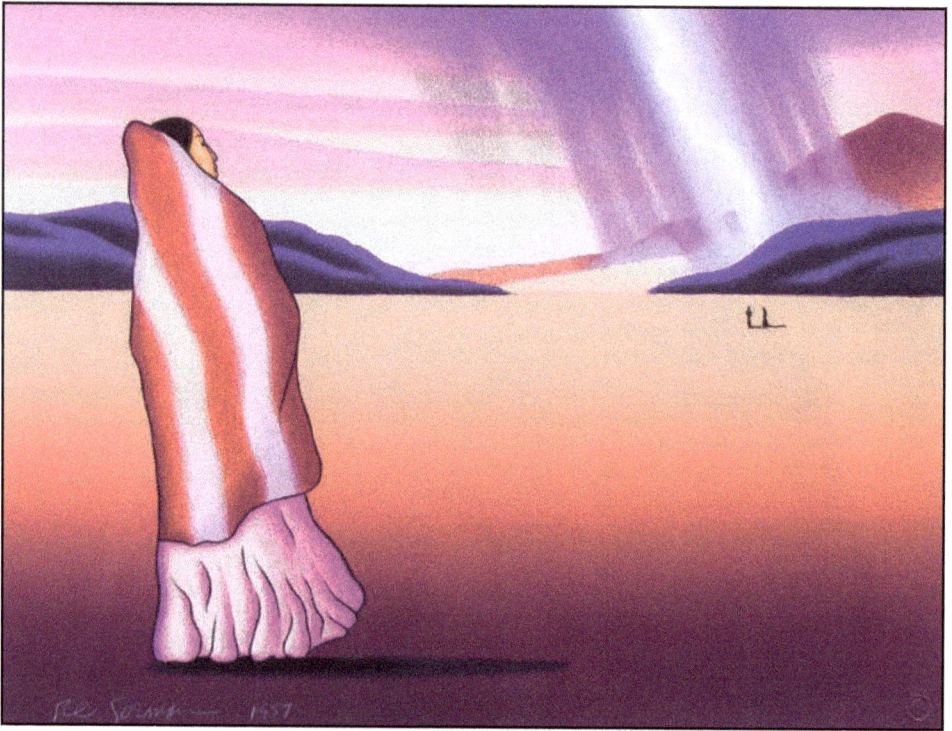

Anniversary Suite - Chuska Storm

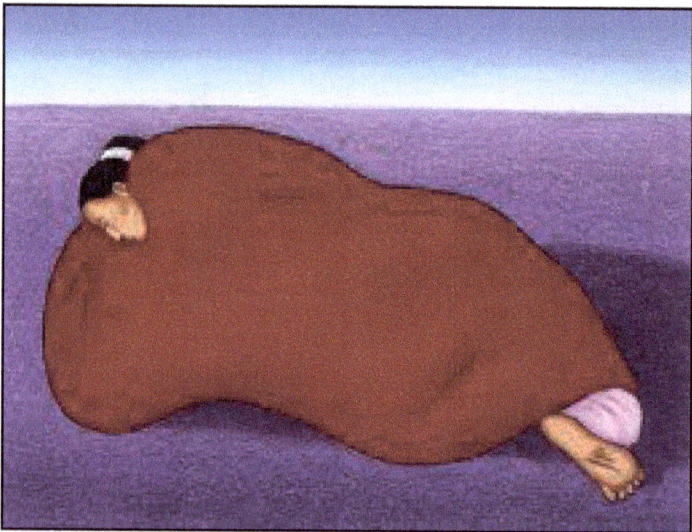

Anniversary Suite - Madrid

Anniversary Suite - Summer

Anniversary Suite - Windsong

Cassandra

Fatima

116

Gracias

Mariposa I

Navajo Velvet

Scarlet I

Tulip Tree

The Blue Gem

16

WOMEN POWER

Four years after his first visit, Gorman returned to Taos to make it his life-long centering place. His love for the city, especially for the Taos Mountains, remained intact for the rest of his life. "The Taos Mountains are my Acropolis, my Pyramids." He used to say.

In Taos, to be successful, it was necessary for him to do what he was good at; networking. To get around and go to different events, he needed a car. But, before getting a car, he had to learn how to drive.

In the past, especially living in San Francisco during the sixties, he would use public transportation or walk. And, while struggling financially, a car was a luxury item.

Now, approaching forty years of age, for the first time in his life, he was looking to buy a used car.

Rosalie Talbot was an establish piano artist. At the young age of six, she studied piano at the University of Tulsa and later on was accepted into the prestigious Juilliard Music School in New York. After performing piano concerts for many years, Rosalie left behind the city life and, in the late sixties, adopted Taos as her home. She desired to be in a superior cultural climate. In Taos, she continued to perform piano concerts in smaller venues until she met R.C. Gorman. She eventually began working for Gorman, managing his Albuquerque gallery and later on she became his home secretary.

Rosalie wanted to sell her old car. R.C. wanted to buy it, but there was that driving problem.

Rosalie offered to be his driving instructor. After the basic instructions on how brakes work, how to accelerate the speed using the gas pedal, and how to maneuver the car, R.C. sat behind the wheel, ready for this new experience. An isolated parking lot was his first driving grounds. Rearview mirror checked, driver's seat adjusted, engine on, gear on drive, and step on the gas. After a rough stop-and-go start, R.C. got used to easing his foot on the gas pedal. He was excited like a little kid getting his first bike. After trying the dirt roads and streets with traffic, R.C. was ready to conquer the highways.

And thus began the legendary driving adventures of R.C. Gorman. Shortly after, R.C. bought a second vehicle, an old van to deliver paintings.

R.C. Gorman's bad driving became legendary. The passenger door of his first Cadillac remained damaged as he tried to maneuver and park the car in the narrow gallery's driveway. The passenger side was dragged against the wall and badly damaged. Gorman ignored the damage completely. When someone asked him, if he was embarrassed driving around town with a damaged car, he answered, "It doesn't bother me. It's on the other side of the driver's door. I don't see it." Gorman was not a good driver at first but, as he did throughout his life, he maintained his good sense of humor.

One time he missed a turn while driving down from a mountain, and landed in the river, luckily it was summer and river was dry. He escaped with an injured left hand. By the time his first Cadillac was loaded with bumps and scratches and he decided to get a new one.

R.C. Gorman, being the generous man he was, often offered his friends and employees a ride, but almost always, people shook their heads and said, "Thanks, I'll walk."

Once R.C. experienced the wonderful world of driving, and as the business was increasing, the Cadillac was replaced by a Lincoln Town Car, and finally a succession of new Mercedes.

Driving might not have been Gorman's best talent and, additionally, he always joked that he was not coordinated enough to do handy work and fix things around the gallery but his ability to single out talents in other people was extraordinary. Like the women he chose to model for him. He instantly recognized their best features.

For some models, he singled out their face, for others the general outline shape of their body. Often, after he would see a woman walking the street or sitting in a restaurant, he would sit in the darkness of his home and mentally draw her.

The models Gorman used for his paintings and sculptures were very different from one another, in size, color and cultural origin and, especially, how they presented themselves.

Most artists use their model's physical image to copy onto their canvas but, surprisingly, not all of Gorman's models were Native American women.

Some were large and round with soft skin, others were tawny-brown and strikingly beautiful. Some had the demeanor of middle eastern princesses, others with an olive Mediterranean skin or graceful oriental origin.

Women, in general, represented an increasingly important aspect of his work. His images on canvas became more and more universal in their appeal. His drawings continued to have the strong ethnic and spiritual look of the Navajo; only the expressions continued to broaden beyond his childhood images of women.

R.C. Gorman made his models feel special. He was a master at bringing out their feminine side without losing their power of expression and individuality. Their inspiration was extremely important for his art.

Beyond physical beauty, he recognized their incredibly beautiful minds and graciousness. He wanted them to act naturally.

Some were quiet, humble, or relaxed. He was attuned to the personality of his model, and he extracted that demeanor to build the images he conceived in his mind and put onto the canvas. The more comfortable he was with them the looser he was in his drawing.

Gorman knew full well that his models set the mood for the piece he was working on, and that the final result of his work would be powerful or expressionless depending on the model's demeanor. If his model was spontaneous, his work was also with an abstract element to it.

If enthusiastic, she would brighten up his canvas.

If the model just had a romantic evening with her mate, there would be an expression of mystique.

If the model was preoccupied with a troubling situation, he would spend hours trying to cheer her up. If he was not able to do so, he would call it a day with her and work on something else.

I met for lunch with one of his models, now in her sixties, married and with children. She is one of the few full-blooded Native American models he used. She wished to remain anonymous and asked to use the name, Alo. I did not ask why since that was none of my business.

This was Alo's response to my first question about Gorman's routine of painting.

"After an initial quick draw, he would often stop and converse with me, and sometimes we'll have a glass of wine and laugh. It was his way of understanding my mood. This was something that was very important to him. Even though I am by nature a happy person, that routine continued for years. It was his way to get me relaxed."

This is what she said about the poses that he liked her to take.

"While we're having fun, he asked me to move and if he liked a pose he would ask me to hold, and he would go back to drawing."

"I understand that he was obsessed with the feet and hands."

She smiled. "Yes, R.C. loved to draw feet and hands – I've always had to show my hands and feet. It was important to him because it was part of his heritage, part of his conception of his art. He wanted to present women who used their feet to work the earth and their hands to make rugs and jewelry.

One of the things I loved about R.C. was that he let me be, so he could capture my natural essence. But, he made my feet look so big. I thought I had to go out and buy size sixteen shoes, after looking at them." She smiled again. Alo seemed comfortable in her skin, confident and extremely happy. I could see why R.C. Gorman loved to work with her.

"How did he direct the entire process?"

"He was a great director. There was no doubt that he was in control. One of the things he taught me was to sit and react like nobody was watching. Then, once I relaxed, he began to draw. Sometimes when I was uncomfortable, he would say. Look there is nobody looking through a keyhole so go back to being natural."

She paused for a moment to reflect on the past. Her eyes seemed to travel back in time. "You know, I don't want to bring up the metaphysical, but the longer I thought about R.C., and the better I got to know the man behind the carefree, gregarious personality he publicly projected, the more I am convinced that there was a spirit that guided his work. He was such a tenacious and gifted practitioner, and when he worked, there were streams of spirituality that poured out unconsciously. There was something transcendent in the way he turned his wrist halfway through a long line. His aesthetic choices of colors were amazing. Sometimes it seemed that his selection of props was random but in fact, it was well thought out about how to add interest to his drawing. Perhaps his public personality was to hide some of the seriousness."

"Did you ever meet with him socially, and if you did, how was it different from working with him?"

"Yes, several times. At first, I was surprised to see his serious side. He was well rounded in all subjects. History, philosophy, religion, his culture, music, which he loved to talk about."

It took me a few moments to digest what she just said. Meantime she stood uncomfortably playing with her fork and food on her plate as if she revealed to the world a secret she had been holding for a while. I decided to move on with the subject. "What about his other models?"

"He worked with a lot of models, but he had a few that were his favorite. One of them was a dancer, when she posed for him she was all theater. Another had a full body and to him she represented the universal woman. The only women he did not like to draw were the skinny women. According to R.C., they didn't fill out the paper."

"I know that you spoke about his ability to communicate but can you elaborate on that?"

"R.C. was a master of psychology. He loved to carry on a conversation with his models, adapting to each model according to their personality and he reacted accordingly. But, when he turned to his canvas, his demeanor changed, he was quiet as if he went to a different space. Unlike his gregarious and fun-loving personality, when at work he isolated his mind, he concentrated on the subject and worked with an insatiable appetite. He was calm while drawing and at the end, some drawings were finished some were unfinished, like notes to a writer. The first part went quickly. But sometimes, unlike the general belief, he took his time to digest the more complex personality of his models, to capture their soul. Once he did, he worked hard and with the flair of a dancer, as if he did not want to lose the thought. There were times that he worked ten to twelve hours on one painting. He works hard and with an unbelievable energy." "What do you think was the main reason for his success?"

"R.C. Gorman went against anyone's formula for success, he was a staunch defender of lower prices, he felt loyalty and an obligation to people who buy his work or the ones who want to. The demand for his work has exploded, so prices do go up but he tried to hold them down." "About his art?"

"It is difficult to define Gorman's art. Let me put it this way.

It is a deep feeling. He has something to say about the strength of women. For some people, that strength is something that is just there, but for R.C. it was a natural deep-rooted expression. Whether talking about his art or his life, and the two are virtually inseparable, he remains indefinable – like his beloved Taos, he was magic."

Navajo women are known for their strength. These earthy, nurturing women work herding sheep, chopping wood, working the fields while having babies. They need to be strong to endure this kind of a lifestyle. It is that essence that Gorman so successfully captured, not the glamorous but the beautiful. His women are at once soft and strong, remote and unpretentious. And, they are not afraid to reveal their strength.

His models were universal, they could be from Arizona, Africa, or the Orient, but they all seemed to be from the reservation. He could make them any way he envisioned them, brown, beautiful, wearing a blanket or working with maze. He created them.

"But, he liked hanging out with the rich and famous," I responded.

"Gorman used to party with the rich, but his work was not designed for them. In many ways, it was designed for those who could not afford it, in many ways for people close to his roots. He often talked about the time he could not afford things, and you see that in how he cared about his family, his concern for the public and the way he collected art. He had some expensive art but most of it was bought from struggling artists, and mostly Native American artists. He used to say that money and fame were not important. Youth is what's important – take advantage of it, use it fully and as passionately as you can for as long as you can. When you are old, you can reflect on it all."

In my last question about the effect, Gorman had in her life.

"I feel special, my confidence to be a good mother and a gracious companion is the biggest asset in my life. It is because of R.C. When you are young, sometimes you look in the mirror and recognize your beauty and with it the danger to become vain. R.C. was the one that taught me to use my beauty to release my feminine power. It has helped me throughout my life. It feels good to be loved but to be respected is a much better and a long-lasting feeling. I do not like to give interviews. One of the reasons for this interview is that one of my friends insisted that I meet with you and that it was time for me to express the graciousness of what R.C. Gorman meant to me."

One last question – do you have any favorites of Gorman's work?

"I love most of his work," she thought for a moment bringing up that calming smile of hers and said, "if you insist on me choosing, *The Navajo Mother and Child,* is one of my favorites. It is a piece that was done in the late seventies."

"What is so special about that piece?"

"Its impact on me is elusive. I tried to analyze it for the longest time. I like the simplicity and peacefulness of it. The mother's sheltering the child, the adoring expression in her black eyes, it projects a fighting motherly feeling, like an animal protecting her baby. Another one is *Dez-bah* done in the early seventies, around the time I started modeling for him. This piece is interesting to me because, although it is the standard concept of Gorman's figure, it seems different in style. The face appeared briefly but abstractly defined. The woman is wrapped in a dazzling yellow robe with impressive red stripes. Those are two of my favorite colors."

I walked away from that meeting feeling her feminine power which, according to her, was the result of working with Gorman.

Another long drive to Scottsdale was ahead of me. Writers have their different ways to process their thoughts. My way is the long drive, especially surrounded by beautiful scenery and my music.

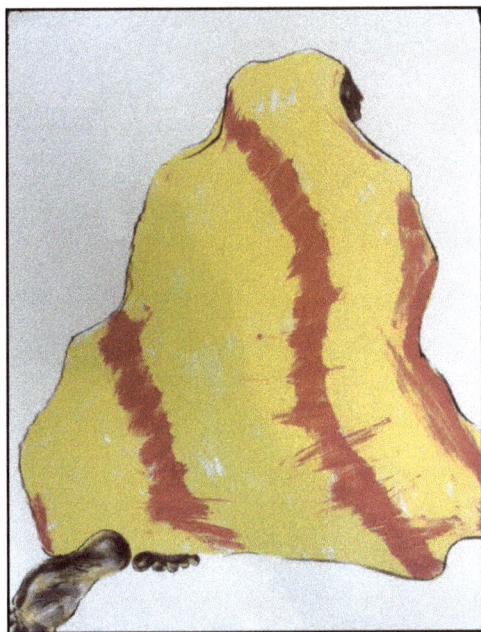

Dez-Bah

Navajo Mother and Child

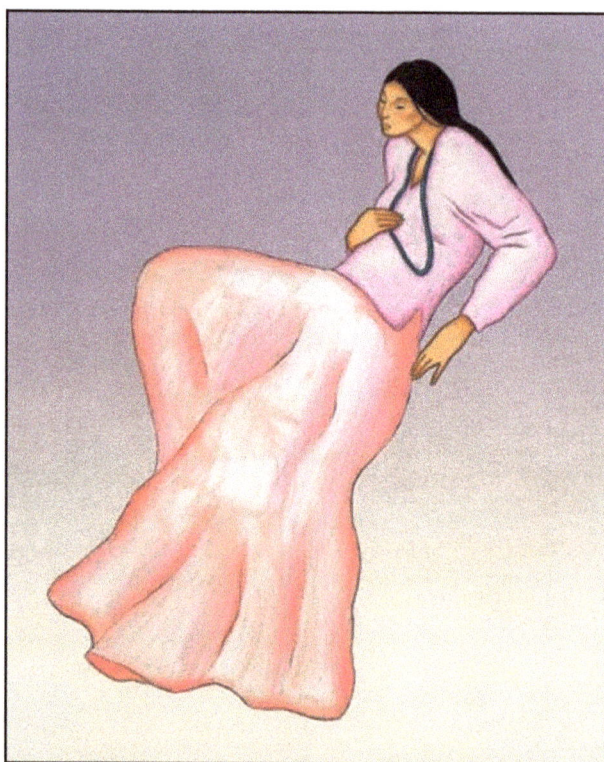

Gala

Moon River

17

TIRELESS TRAVELS

Gorman loved to travel, not the reclusive and nearly spiritual experience I feel driving along the highways, but the clamorous and engaged style of first class. Anyone who traveled with Gorman would tell you that the pace he kept was exhausting. He would talk, joke, and laugh. He would drink, eat and celebrate life. He would also write or draw on a thick, medium size black book he always carried with him.

Since the days when little Rudy walked home from school about three miles away, he craved knowledge about the world outside the reservation. When he came home from school and had to chop wood or milk the goats, he wondered about neighborhoods he has seen in books. He wondered about tall buildings, cars and children playing in the streets.

In the summers Rudy, would sometimes stay with his grandmother Alice or go into the town of Kaibito, to help his father.

Rudy loved herding sheep, being outside in nature and picking herbs and fruits alongside his beloved grandmother. They would eat wild berries, homemade cheese and drink fresh milk.

For little Rudy, grandma's home was in a magical place. At night they would sit outside, glance at the clear sky, dotted with myriads of stars, and his grandmother would tell Rudy the names of the stars and their constellations.

She told him about Polaris, also known as the North Star, a bright star in the night sky, and how this has been used as a navigational tool for people since ancient times.

His Grandmother was wise and had knowledge about other cultures and stories of long ago. She told him about the Seven Sisters of the Pleiades, an open star cluster located in the constellation of Taurus. She told him a story about the famous Aquarius, one of the biggest constellations, named after a very handsome young man who served the gods. Recognizing his service, Zeus granted eternal youth to this young man.

In the southern summer sky, there was the constellation of the Milky Way, within it there was Aquila, the head and wings of the eagle who used to live in Mount Olympus. The eagle is a great symbol of courage, wisdom and strength for the Navajo people. There was Aries, the ram whose fleece became the Golden Fleece, and sailors sailed to the ends of the earth to find it. For the Navajos, the ram symbolized their backbone, survival and their lifeline. Grandma knew them all.

Around grandmother's house, there was a place to swim; an open river, lined with bars of big rocks and running clear, cool water. Rudy loved to swim there and, since he did not have the luxury of a swimming suit, he would dive in the nude. There were places to daydream and places to play. There was wildlife, and tall ponderosa pine, fir, juniper and sagebrush surrounding this pristine area. When summer was over, they would ride grandma's white donkey back home to Chinle, over twenty miles away. The road back was full of dramatic sandstone cliffs, mysterious fossils, and fleeting remnants of Navajo petroglyphs and pictographs. Grandmother would point out plants that had medicinal powers and she would pick the beautiful flowers. One time she picked a lily flower and pointed out the beauty of it. His grandmother said that the earth gives us food to eat, but some of it is poisonous, like this beautiful flower. She compared it to people; some people might be beautiful and vindictive at the same time. "We are privileged to be allowed to live in this beautiful land," grandmother would often say.

His father, Carl, was working for the government in the city of

Kaibito. He was paid to brand cattle and to sheer sheep; it was hard work.

When Rudy spent the summers with his father, it was a different adventure from that of his grandmother. Rudy always felt bad leaving his mother and his younger siblings behind. He and his dad always made sure that the family had enough supplies while they were away. In Kaibito, he would help his father brand cattle. They would cook, eat outside, and draw with the crayons his father bought for him. His father taught him to respect nature and all people, he spoke about the world where many people were poor and hungry. He spoke about wars. He told Rudy that if he wanted to help people, he had to learn how to speak the English language. Rudy learned to work hard next to his dad, and he also experienced another side of his father; gambling. The working men would sit around the table, drink, and play cards, they would throw their hard-earned money on the table. His dad was joyful when he won and moody when he lost.

One summer his dad gave Rudy a surprise gift- a bicycle. Rudy was overcome with excitement; it was one of the happiest moments of his life. He rode the bike around and asked the Navajo girls to pose for him so he could draw them. They were his first models.

Once he was famous, R.C remembered his father's words about helping people and he was glad to take time off his hectic schedule and do fundraising for the arts. He often helped the Santa Fe Opera, The Heard Museum, the Phoenix Art Museum, and the Albuquerque Museum, raise money to keep the arts alive.

In one of his appearances, before the evening's fundraising event at the Phoenix Art Museum, along with Virginia, and Lee, one of his adopted sons, visited his friend Dr. Byron Butler.

Dr. Butler was a Native American art collector. He collected rugs, old baskets, masks, and he was interested in American Indian contemporary work. Years ago, when Dr. Butler was visiting a friend's home he saw a painting on his wall. The signature read R.C. Gorman. He had never heard of him, but he liked his art. Dr. Butler traveled to San Francisco looking for R.C. Gorman's apartment. He found his building, walked several flights up and found him. Dr. Butler found a skinny, hungry kid with a tremendous sense of humor and felt obligated to take him to dinner. After dinner, he returned to Phoenix carrying several of Gorman's drawings.

Dr. Butler eventually became the financial backer for R.C. Gorman's lithographs for several years to come.

Gorman, Virginia, and Lee sat in the spacious living room, overlooking Camelback mountain. Dr. Butler appeared frail, seemingly not in good health. The demeanor of Gorman, once in the company of Dr. Butler, completely changed. There was no jokes and frivolousness. Gorman was subdued and treated Dr. Butler with utmost respect.

Besides practicing medicine, Dr. Butler had an Art Consulting Business. It was the vehicle of his art consulting that propelled some of the sales of Gorman's paintings and lithographs.

Dr. Butler's exhibit of collections of Native American art which was predominately Gorman was shown at the Heard Museum, in Tulsa center of the arts, and in the museum in Northern Arizona in Flagstaff.

It was Dr. Butler's idea to work with the Tamarind Institute, located in Los Angeles back in the sixties. This was a turning point of Gorman's life.

One copy of his first lithograph is displayed in the Department of Bureau of The Indian Affairs in Washington DC.

Dr. Butler visited the Tamarind Institute and talked with its founder June Wayne whose vision was to revive the medium of lithography by training master printers to adopt new technologies and to entice artists to join forces and make lithographs by working with highly qualified master printers.

The Tamarind Institute is credited with reviving interest in lithography as an art medium by their dedicated research for technological breakthroughs.

One of the principal goals of the Tamarind Institute, since its creation in 1960, was to develop a long relationship with artists and to help them become masters of lithography.

Until the early sixties, lithography was unknown to the wider public. The first lithographic images were yellowed and darkened etchings.

With R.C. Gorman's involvement and Tamarind's advance technology, the images began to change rapidly. The dynamic collaboration between Tamarind's master printers and R.C. Gorman played critical roles in an explosion of lithography and the madness that followed among artists and collectors for limited edition prints.

Gorman's earlier Tamarind prints were simply black and white line drawings, the occasional monochromatic background was added to dramatize the figure. Slowly the lithographs became more colorful and graceful.

Gorman continued to work with the Tamarind Institute after it moved to Albuquerque and the University of New Mexico, in 1970. By now, Tamarind trained master printers were moving out and spreading the art around the country. There were shops in Houston, San Francisco and Tubac, Arizona. These were places where Gorman, eventually worked with their printers.

With R.C. Gorman's involvement, lithography became a popular medium. Without exaggeration, Gorman is more responsible than any other artist for the populism of limited edition prints in America.

The audience of his images were vast and through his tenacious determination and capacity for tireless work, his skills and the use of master printers; he made available his art for those who wanted it at a price they could afford.

The first series produced by R.C. Gorman in Tamarind was *Homage to Navajo Women*, a suite of five lithographs. The production that included, *Corn Mother, Noon Meditation, Mother and Child, Walking Women, and Navajo Woman,* was limited to seventy impressions.

Homage to Navajo Women became a book, published by Art Consultants, Dr. Butler's company in collaboration with the Tamarind Institute.

Over their years of working with Gorman, lithography printers have made great technical strides. They have effective techniques to create rich textural Gorman's figures. The difference between the first lithographs of the *Homage to Navajo Women,* and the colors of the ones years later are stunning, like in *Tortilla Maker* in 1978, *Amelia* in the eighties, and later in

Wild Flowers, in the nineties. Though Gorman's work had evolved, so did the color quality as well, it was becoming far more superior. The blending of the colors in this extremely complex process of lithography and the techniques to creating these effects could be only accomplished by the relationship of extremely talented artist and superior skillful printers.

Corn Mother

Noon Meditation

Mother and Child

Walking Women

136

Navajo Women

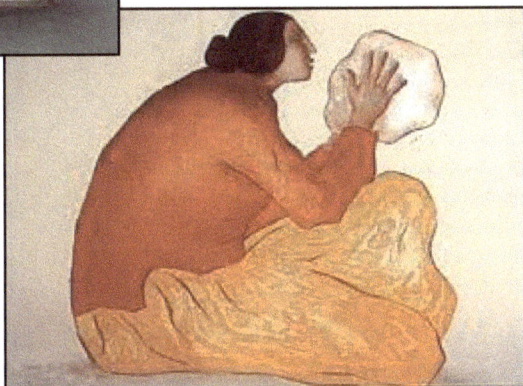

Tortilla Maker

Wild Flowers

Amelia

Another reason that the process had become more complex is that Gorman kept adding more colors to his images. Gorman eventually used over eighty colors. This multiple array of colors required the printers to use several different stones and plates for production. Gorman's work could be found in several national museum collections, including the Metropolitan Museum of Art in New York City, where R.C. Gorman's appearance in 1983, was a milestone. He was the only living artist to be included in the showing, *"Masterworks of the Native Americans."*

The museum's management was so amazed at Gorman's work that they purchased two drawings from the exhibit. The New York Times art editorial staff named him, *"The Picasso of American Indian art."*

R.C. Gorman's art hero was Picasso, along with Michelangelo and Rembrandt. To be in the same sentence with these masters was not only an emotional moment for him but a motive to live up to the accolade.

The following years he worked hard. He traveled cross-country to do endless showings. His was now producing more work than ever. The grueling travel schedule exhausted everyone, except Gorman, who was animated with his success.

There were trips to Japan to do a rare series of woodblocks, now treasured by collectors. The numerous tours of Europe for exhibitions and printing projects in France, Germany, Italy, Spain, and Greece.

His international clientele increased with each appearance. His scheduled exhibits from Palm Springs, to Honolulu, to Australia and many cities in between.

He did a European tour with his sister, Donna, and he took the time to produce a lithograph at the *Lithografia R. Bulla* press in Rome.

He visited the Harvard University to receive a Humanitarian Award. This award motivated him to start an annual scholarship for Taos High School students of Native American and Hispanic descent. He was honored for being the first artist chosen for a series of one-man exhibitions of contemporary Indian artists held in the Museum of the American Indian and drew a record attendance.

Next he went to Hindenburg Germany, invited by his friend Chrisa Nazinger, to do a showing in her gallery. It was a different experience for Gorman. The mayor of the town was there to give a speech, and as the attendants applauded, Gorman waived, not even knowing what they were applauding for since he spoke no German.

Earlier, Gorman filmed the first of many TV documentaries in PBS. The six half-hour programs, entitled *"American Indian Artists,"* presented a memorable cast of Native American artists, among them was R.C. Gorman.

There was the Smithsonian's National Museum of the American

Indian exhibition, highlighting twenty-eight of Gorman's early works of his *Indian Madonnas*. In that event, Gorman displayed charm and humor. He insisted that the museum would exhibit a rare self-portrait featuring his trademark headband and wearing sunglasses. It was a drawing that Gorman poked fun at himself with his Navajo headband, modern American shades, unshaven and with a Mexican looking mustache. He had a broken pattern of turquoise beads hanging over a pink shirt. His other works included several nudes, among them the oil pastel *"Navajo Woman Drying Her Hair,"* This was a bold, sensuous image of a standing woman touching her hair, charged with sexual excitement, reminiscent of Degas' series of his *Bathing Women.*

Woman Drying her hair

Self Portrait

He did a show in Tubac's Center for the Arts. He loved the city's blend of cultures of Mexicans and Native Americans and he decided to open a gallery there. When he opened the gallery in Tubac, Arizona, an art community between Tucson and the Mexican borders, Gorman was himself, excited, cracking jokes, and being Gorman.

Between his exhibits, charity work, workshops and interviews he had to satisfy his starving appetite for authentic food and traveled for osso buco in Italy, paella and raw ham in Spain, and for calamari in Greece. But, despite his travels around the world and the myriads of unique tastes he experienced, he always went back to the reservation for his Aunt Mary's blood sausages.

I am already exhausted writing about his travels. But, wait. There were more!

R.C. Gorman did not like to make long plans. He did not seem to worry much about the future; he loved spontaneity. The only sight he did not want to see was retirement.

The haunting question, "What is this Indian doing in the white man's world?" surfaced again in one of his trips to Chicago. He was there for a week to do a showing. It was the first night, after a party in his honor, returned to the hotel. He wore his trademark headband and a nice suit. The doorman of the luxurious Hyatt Regency stopped him and asked if he was staying there. As usual, Gorman was polite, he showed the man his room key, but the doorman was still skeptical. After a few minutes, the doorman insisted that he could only go in if he took off his headband, Gorman smiled, told the doorman that was not going to happen and walked by the doorman who tried to stop him. He went up to his room, checked out, and then checked into the Ritz Carlton.

Gorman kept up his work, and if someone invited him to a party, and many times people did, in Rome, in Madrid or Acapulco, he was there.

In Antibes, a resort town in southwest France, built upon the foundation of the ancient Greek town of Antipolis, there is a Picasso museum. R.C. Gorman visited the museum often. It was one of his favorite places.

He also liked to visit another Picasso museum in Barcelona. Gorman claimed that Picasso inspired him to work more on ceramics.

During my research, I was reading through the many television appearances of R.C. Gorman, ...Good Morning America, The Jane Pauley Show...The Rita Davenport Cooking Show... Wait. What. I was on Rita's show many times when I was a professional chef in the mid-eighties. Our paths have crossed after all.

R.C. Gorman travelled far searching for his golden fleece – he founded it in Taos.

He, no longer, had to watch the jets coming and going in the San Francisco airport, nor did he have to share a beer with his buddies. He could now get on any jet plane he wanted and drink expensive wines. He earned this.

Amelia

Aunt Eta

Las Palomas

18

MIXED FEELINGS

Friendship is a peculiar claim.

A few of Gorman's friends, after his death, started the backstabbing. Some of his old friends called him crazy, unstable and greedy, one of them even claimed that he painted the works of art, not Gorman. Personally, I have no respect for people talking trash about someone that has passed away and cannot defend himself, especially when this dead person's work put food on their table and paid their mortgage.

Admittedly, those who used criticism as their weapon were very few, but it is an issue worth addressing. I strongly believe that no one can copy someone's work to perfection. It is close to an impossibility, especially for artists who the public knows their art well.

It is like saying that Sinatra could not sing, so someone did it for him. And, no one noticed! There is no way to imitate that beautiful tone with the extraordinary fullness that is cool, and yet so laid back. I mean, really! Especially when he runs out of lyrics and sings, *Dooby dooby doo*. Who could do that?

Or that anyone would be able to play Marlon Brando's character in *The Godfather*. No one would be able to grimace those chilling facial expressions, or talk with that rasping, terrifying voice, *"I'll make him an offer he can't refuse."* There is no way to re-create that one.

I get it – I too, like to think that in my past lives I wrote Dostoevsky's *Crime and Punishment* and Tolstoy's *War and Peace,* but that is a laughable, as well an elusive dream.

Believe me, I tried to play soccer like Pele, but I could never master that scissor kick of his – I always fell flat on my back.

And I tried to cook like my father, but I did not even come close.

Consequently, what I can do is scramble a few words on paper hoping to make sense. At the end of the day my storytelling might not be, and I am sure it is not, the best, but at least it is mine.

However, my writing style is influenced by my literary heroes, Kazantzakis, and Oriana Fallaci. I love his deep, passionate wisdom and the fearless honesty in her tenacious lines, but it would be sacrilegious to claim that I write like them.

Admittedly or not we are influenced by others. It is one thing to be influenced by someone you admire and another to pretend that you are him or her. Gorman had as many people trying to imitate his art, as Elvis had impersonators, especially after his death. That is a great credit to his art.

In my humble opinion, the art community needs to get over the old tired beliefs that great art is intended only for the few.

There are many people that would like to have a Van Gogh, or a Rembrandt, hanging on their wall. There is only a handful of people who have the ability to pay millions to get one of those pieces.

So, the eternal question remains; what is wrong with some limited editions or even copies signed by the artist for all people to enjoy?

It is like saying that the Rolling Stones made one copy of *Satisfaction* and sold it for millions so only one person would be able to listen to it.

Or J.K. Rowling printed one copy of *Harry Potter* and auctioned for the highest bid, for only one kid to read it.

 Or if there was only one person allowed to view *Gone With the Wind.* Gorman was one of the pioneers who made limited edition copies and, later on, prints of his art. I am certain that the reason that Gorman was so adamant about mass-producing his pieces was for more people to enjoy them.

It is also the reason that I believe his art will touch generations to come while other great pieces of art will have limited viewers in some museum or isolated in someone's room and reserved for art's high society crowd.

One of my passions is to help new authors to improve their writing skills before moving forward with the publishing of their work.

In one of my writing sessions with Dr. John, I noticed two Gorman pieces on his wall. It was the time when I began the writing of Gorman's book.

When Mary, his wife, walked into the room, I asked her about the Gorman pieces.

"We love them," she said.

One of the pieces was *Anabah*, a long-drawn body, covered in a white dress. Unmistakable was Gorman's signature long curved lines and the large brown feet. The other was, *Navajo Mother in Law*, an older woman, hands on hips and face turned with a disgusted expression. It captures the prototypical characteristic of a mother's disapproval of the treatment of her son.

I looked at Mary and smiled, "Really, Ms. Mary?"

She shook her head, eyes wide opened, lips put together, "No, no, I loved my mother-in-law." Dr. John nodded his head in agreement with his wife.

"Our children are arguing about who is going to inherit these pieces," Mary said smiling.

So, there you have it. Children who were toddlers when Gorman passed, want his art.

Anabah

Navajo Mother in Law

And there is the "lazy myth". Lazy? Seriously!

R.C. Gorman's output of work is incomprehensible for anyone who knows what it takes to produce art. His art production includes hundreds of lithographs, original paintings, drawings, etchings, tapestries, ceramics, bronzes, sculptures, woodblocks, and every type of medium that he could get his hands on. Tens of thousands of impressions printed. Gorman has the second most prolific production of printed art, right behind Pablo Picasso.

To be clear, Gorman is no Picasso but looking back it is difficult to find another artist with a greater appetite to make art.

I am amazed that art historians, outside of the southwest, have paid very little attention to R.C. Gorman. However, that neglect has done nothing to slow down his fame, in fact, the opposite may be true.

A collector of rare art that I know told me once that those who buy Gorman's lithographs are not real collectors, they know nothing about art. Those who buy his originals are the real art lovers.

I said to him, "My friend, it is not that confusing. You see a piece of art; you like it, you can afford it, you buy it – that simple."

He looked at me and smiled, "That is not how art collection works. Art loses its value and splendor once reproduced."

"Look, some of us would not know a Van Gogh or a Da Vinci from a nice -looking painting bought at a garage sale. It might turn off an art collector, but there are those who like to see it hanging on their wall."

I was helping a lady with her writing. Every time I went to her upscale home, she takes me on tour to show me her valuable art. Showing me her work is an ego boost for her. I am sure she enjoys her art, but I don't. Every time I visit her home, the routine continues. My unconcerned reaction is not enough to send her the message that this is a boring tour – enough already.

There is my buddy, Albert, an elderly gentleman in his mid-eighties. I visit him often to make sure he is okay. I stay for a while so he can read me his poetry. Albert's little home is full of art, I mean every inch of his walls is covered with art. Some of his art is a bit expensive, but most of it is not. However, he loves it. Every morning he gets up, he looks at his walls and feels like a king – that is what art is meant to do for people.

My friend, Albert, writes great poetry. I've always been intrigued by creative individuals, especially artists, writers, songwriters, and poets.

I know many so-called "starving artists" who sit on volumes of worthwhile unpublished work, waiting for their chance to shine. The general reaction to struggling artists is sympathy, but when they are successful, they become subjects of spitefulness - I don't get it.

During my research for this book, I've watched endless videos of Gorman and other artists at work. Many artists have stiff, short strokes, they think for a while, then create, correct and recreate. Gorman, on the other hand, is full of energy, he is like a dancer, constantly moving. Both of his hands are agitated like the hands of a violinist. He talks with his model, directs her to move, to turn, to hold. He acts and reacts; he smiles, he frowns, he shakes his head. His painting hand detailing the face, quickly, precisely, then he draws his trademark long curving lines, and the moment he breaks his wrist to curve those lines, there is magic. I could see why people loved to watch him at work.

Yes, Gorman was a bit eccentric. But here a secret: there is a long list of great artists who are eccentric.

Many plants and flowers are poisonous; the grandmother told him when she picked that beautiful lily flower. Gorman always remembered that and he wasn't bothered when someone bad-mouthed him. Yes, he made mistakes as all of us do, but the mistakes are not who we are. Defiling someone's life who, during his time on earth gave us gifts of beauty, is downright nasty. It should be a lesson for us to learn not to pay attention to the part of our community that judges and does not forgive.

R.C. Gorman was called brilliant, the pride of Navajo Nation, a genius. Others call him arrogant, flamboyant, and crazy.

But there is no disagreement about his talent. His free-flowing style was as unrestrained as the water stream he swam when a little boy. His color sense was as elusive as the spectacular display of colors in his beloved New Mexico open sky on a fall sunset. This is where, from the top to bottom along the western horizon, the colors unfolded from blush lavender into deep pink and golden yellow, creating glowing visual glory of colors.

19

NEW HOME

Besides the classic Navajo and Anglo reads for children in the small elementary school library in Chinle, Rudy was surprised to find some very unusual books. Those were books from the tales of *One Thousand and One Nights*. He was intrigued by the wonderful stories of strange faraway places. There were flying carpets, magic lamps, and a sailor searching for adventures. Throughout the pages, there were stories about a luxurious palace and tables ladened with food. There were silks, diamonds and rubies, and unusual names like Ali Baba and many other names that his young tongue was overwhelmed trying to pronounce.

Young Rudy was mesmerized. Some days, during the long walks to his home from school, he was sure that he saw mirages. He saw oases with palm trees, images of sand dunes, men on horses, swords, and magic rocks. The omnipresent ancient ruins in the canyon at the bottom of the tall rock formation had become an imaginary palace where Scheherazade and Shahryan spent their mythical days.

Over forty years passed for R.C. since those magical days. So much happened. Just in the past decade; People can communicate with email, there are laser printers, and pocket calculators.

Music is changing; progressive rock, Genesis, Zeppelin, Queen, Bowie. The Beatles break up, Elvis dies.

More channels and new shows on television, Happy Days, Columbo, Kojak, Roots.

Blockbuster movies, The Exorcist, Jaws, and Star Wars.

Momentous moments in sports: Secretariat wins the Triple Crown, Hank Aaron breaks Babe Ruth's record, Old man Ali knocks down Foreman, Magic facing Bird.

Many historical events have taken place, Apollo 13 returns to earth, Kent State massacre, gay rights movement, energy crisis, Watergate, Cambodia genocide, Iran hostage crisis. And there is a new saint; Mother Teresa wins the Nobel Prize.

R.C. Gorman was about to change as well. After eleven years on Ledoux Street, he was now ready to move.

The place on Ledoux Street was perfect for a gallery, but as living quarters it was getting crowded. More employees were working in the gallery by now. Besides Virginia, and Rosalie, there were several other helpers and assistants, responsible for helping Gorman, to keep inventory, travel with Gorman, and handle sales and shipment of artwork.

Gorman, remembering the unpleasant experiences he had with brokers and agents, he felt safer when he was in control and surrounded with people he trusted.

The customer traffic was ongoing during the day while the parties and special events were happening almost nightly. There were just a few moments of privacy. Gorman needed more room, for his alone time and more space to create his art and to display his art collection.

There was an Adobe fixer-upper, just north of Taos with a full view of the Mountains. The house needed a lot of work, but the full view of the mountains was of most importance for Gorman.

The first thing was for Gorman to create his new studio. It needed to be much more spacious and private. There was a long swimming pool, a nice guest house, a modern kitchen, a library, a large living room showcasing a grand Steinway piano. There was even a dressing room for the models, and of course, there was a garden.

The final result was a stunning home that some people called it

Gorman's Palace others call it Fort Gorman. The new home was filled with a great amount of privacy and a sweeping panoramic view. His bedroom was designed in a way that the first thing he saw in the morning was the mountains.

And so, moving out from Ledoux Street, the era of romanticism came to an end. No longer would the artist be sleeping on a cot in a place overpowering by odors of oil paints, linseed oil, and lanolin paint. The easels, frames and canvases, and brushes were no longer by the bed. Nor were the drawing pencils and palette knives scattered everywhere.

Another era began, one that he imagined long ago, walking home from school, after reading those mystical books. And why not? He worked hard for it.

But the question remained. Is this new lifestyle going to affect his work?

At this stage of his career, Gorman did not work by routine; he simply painted when he was inspired. He was self-contained in his new home, where he was surrounded by art, it gave him great pleasure. The art he collected was art that he liked, not necessary a piece done by a famous artist. Most of the pieces hanging on his walls were by promising young artists. There was also a Joan Miro, a few Picasso, and a Chagall.

Gorman maintained his philosophy that other people were trained to do work that he wasn't good at. Besides, there were plenty of people that needed to earn money and he was happy to provide work for them. He also claimed that he was aware of what was happening around him, but, as we would see later on, his confidence of controlling everything was questionable.

One thing that was unquestionable though, was that R.C. Gorman single-handedly made it vogue to be a Native American artist.

And he was proud of being a Native American Artist. He maintained his position that he had nothing to prove, he wanted to live his way and to keep his Navajo attitudes.

The reservation was his source of inspiration and what he painted was influenced by his culture. Gorman strongly believed that someday the culture would be obliterated by integration and all will be lost forever. The traditional crafts and arts of Native American influence would only be found in some museum. He wanted to preserve his culture treasures.

Gorman was aware of history and he had a gift but he knew he wasn't the only gifted person. Therefore, he was thankful that his background and talent provided him with a good life and let him explore the world beyond the Navajo reservation.

He had walked in shoes that were beyond repair and outgrown by his feet. He went to Sunday mass with his mother, while wearing shredded pants and worn out shirts.

He did not feel guilty walking through the pair of lion statues standing guard by his front door, opening his heavy library door to look at the plethora of books about art history, philosophy, and cookbooks. His garden was graced with bronze sculptures, his indoor swimming pool surrounded by greenery, satiric sculptures, and an abundance of sunshine filtering through the skylight. His gallery room was filled with oil pastel originals, lithographs, paper casts and posters from every decade of his prolific career. He loved to look at his father's large picture which he hung above the fireplace. One of his prized possessions was a couple of pieces of Larry Bell, who Gorman considered a genius and the Sergio Bustamante's large rhinoceros. There hung a red ink painting of a Kachina by Fritz Scholder, and there was a collection of Kachina dolls and elephants from India

His permanent companions were two fat cats, Lola and Maria. One black, the other white who spent the day laying on his fur covered couch.

I don't get it - Why should he feel guilty?

He wasn't the only artist that made it big. Superstar artists left behind estates worth millions, among them O'Keeffe, Dali, Warhol, Bacon, Willem de Kooning, Rothko, Michelangelo, Picasso, and some like Rembrandt, made millions but ended up bankrupt because of their spending habits.

Gorman wasn't the one to go small. He wanted to enjoy life while he was still on earth – more power to him.

The obvious question is; does he ever think back to the days when he did not have an indoor toilet or new clothes to wear?

Wealth for any dedicated artist is a curious subject. Some are oblivious to the public response and go on enjoying life, others, like Gorman, deal with the guilty feeling of having a lot of money by donating to charity and earmarking certain profits to aid young students.

He did contribute much more than the public would ever know because he did not feel the need to promote his charitable self.

He did not find it necessary to brag about it, but many of those who have been touched by his kindness are not silent about his legendary sincerity of giving.

Rose, his housekeeper, and cook made his home wonderful, and all of his guests were treated alike by her.

She liked to shop for Gorman's favorite foods every morning. She would return home to prepare lunch and dinner. Gorman enjoyed helping in the kitchen sometimes, but most of the time he would sit and watch Rose cook – it was one of his best entertainments.

Rose always prepared food on Gorman's birthday. Everyone was invited.

In the earlier years, Gorman's entire family would travel to Taos to celebrate his birthday and he encouraged them to stay longer. It was a time when the kitchen would be full of people trying to help. Those were glorious days full of laughter and tradition.

It also kept Gorman grounded.

The one person that always kept him grounded was his aunt Mary. She was a creative woman. There was nothing she could not do. She was a great cook, she could repair just about anything, she even built her own home. She also did clay molding and herded sheep. She always gave R.C. handmade gifts, such as rugs and jewelry. Sometimes she would dig a little pit in the yard, light a fire and roast sheep meat. She knew how much R.C. loved it and that was her gift to him. When Gorman watched his aunt doing that, he knew that the big house, the fancy cars, meant nothing to her. She would keep reminding him about the reservation which brought him back to perspective.

Beauty Way

Canyon De Chelly

Expectation

Calabasas

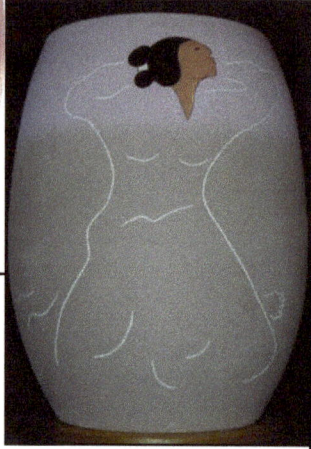

Daydreamers

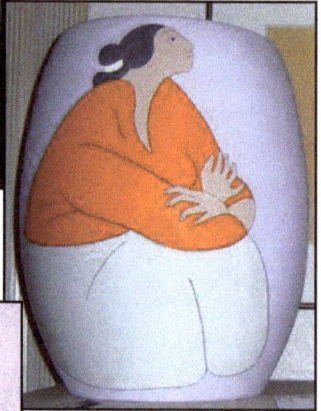

Lea

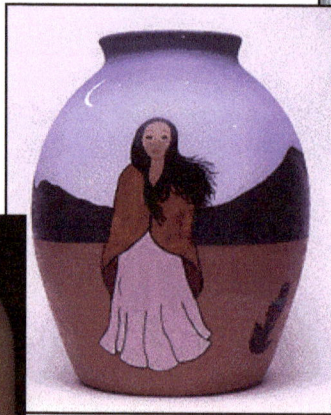

Luna

Rita

20

TRAILS OF TIME

A gold Mercedes was speeding along the dirt roads of Taos. The driver was wearing a red bandana, and a colorful Hawaiian shirt.

Some days, R.C. Gorman would be awake before sunrise, to get away from the house, to be with nature, to reflect. The hectic pace was catching up with him, and mortality was slowly crawling into his mind. Not too long ago his gallbladder became infected and burst. After a major surgery and a long recovery, he was back at work. He was now preaching to others; do not poison yourself, steer clear of alcohol. Gorman never smoked, but alcohol was his permanent companion throughout his life. Now he was drinking less, mostly wine but the damage was done.

Occasionally, he liked to go on to the deserted roads, to be around his beloved mountains, to drive fast, to see as much as possible for a short time.

He enjoyed driving through the cottonwoods. He felt that the trees were slowly disappearing and being replaced with buildings and busy roads.

The dirt roads were reminiscent of his childhood in Chinle and the cottonwoods of grandma's magical place.

His music, from the fifties, mingled with the chirping of birds that flitted from tree to tree. It was a joyous sound over the smooth humming of the motor.

The furious voice of his teacher in Chinle public school, broke into his thoughts, overwhelming the gentle wind whispering between the treetops. He was remembering the time when his teacher was walking around, checking students work and saw his drawing of the naked lady. He could not understand why he was taken to the corner of the room and spanked, but he was glad that this incident did not derail him from his vision.

He thought of his mother. She was no longer alive, but she was the one who took care of him. His father just dropped in from time to time. Was it wrong to make his father his hero?

He did not like seeing his younger nieces and nephews sitting around watching television and not using his library full of helpful books. The things he wanted to be remembered by was his hard work and that he was someone who cared about people. He wanted to be an example. If this little-barefooted boy who used to herd sheep in the black mountains made it in the white men's world, anyone coming from the same background could be comfortable in both worlds.

He was nervous when people confronted him with the question about what he was doing for his people. If people could not see what he was doing for his people that was their problem.

He has helped many of his nieces and nephews. He was a godfather to many children.

He adopted Rose and Virginia as his mothers and adopted many to be his sons, Lee and Jamaica, among them. He helped many other artists and he put kids through school.

He smiled about his old beat up car – now he was driving a gold Mercedes. There was that defining trip from San Francisco to Taos, his first gallery, the times of celebration there and his art. It all seemed like a dream.

All his true friends were in Taos– struggling artists, musicians, actors, poets; he related to them. He wanted to create a cemetery for artists in his estate, so that he would be surrounded in eternity by other artists.

He was amused that he was called Picasso. He was certain that the master was turning in his grave.

The sun came out again, casting slanted beams of light across the mountains. The sun rays slowly climbed over the mountains and reflected between the tall trees. It was an image straight out of heaven, and it stayed with him all the way home.

His mother thought that he was dead once, but his grandmother smacked him back to life. The occasional car speeding through the country roads was a reminder of feeling alive.

He sometimes questioned success but it was a fleeting thought. He was amazed at what was happening to him. He wanted to be successful but this level of notoriety? He never thought that it would happen.

There were temporary dry spells. But now he could afford it. It was different when he was young, charged up and always working.

There is a trail in the Grand Canyon called, *Trail of Time.*

Its entrance is on the south rim of the canyon, through the Yavapai Museum. Yavapai, is another Native American tribe, literally meaning People of The Sun. The Yavapai County is next to Flagstaff, a town where R. C. Gorman first saw the sun of the new world. The views tracking through the trail are magnificent. This trail takes you through billions of years of layers of geology that make up the wonder called the Grand Canyon. There are wildlife and numerous trees along the breathless geology that unfolds in front of your eyes. The end of the trail, about three miles long, is at the Maricopa Point and on to the new world. This trail is symbolic of R.C. Gorman's life.

His trails so far were lengthy, challenging and rewarding. He had seen many cultures since the days of the long past when he first met men in the navy coming from different cultural backgrounds. Men clad in bell bottoms with that distinctive Old Spice smell, drinking Schlitz beer and screwdrivers.

Many years later, after his passing, he was buried on his estate. Soon after, a charter school bought his beautiful home. The doors and stained-glass windows, light fixtures and everything of value was taken out and sold. Statues destroyed, windows broken, the garden dried out until the school went bankrupt. A plundered mansion was left behind.

Various animals infested the property. There were colonies of prairie dogs, mice, squirrels, and pigeons.

The pair of lions standing guards were ravaged and unable to protect the once beautiful place. Pink slime and white mold covered the swimming pool's water and the grass had grown so tall that it was covered the statue around the pool.

Nothing remained of the glory days, the parties and the celebrities. It became a long-faded memory. The kitchen where great aromas of foods escaped now they were reduced to stale smells.

More than one person in Taos told me that it is a shame how Gorman's house was let go, this place should have been Taos' Graceland.

21

ROMANCING THE METAL

R.C. Gorman slowed his frantic pace of the lithograph prints when he entered the decade of the nineties and started the production of various bronze sculptures. Although he did bronzes earlier in his career, this was an attempt at a more prolific presentation.

Gorman was over sixty years old and it was becoming more difficult to keep up with the rigorous pace of production of the lithographs. Even though the process of finalizing bronze sculptures is one of the most complicated methods of art, Gorman could set up a slower pace and sculpt the clay models in his studio over several months.

The first known casting of metal is dated back to China in the fourth century BC. Since then, metal casting has become a popular industry worldwide. In the United States, foundries were a big part of the American industrial revolution during the mid-eighteen-hundreds. It contributed to one of the most important times in the economic development of the United States.

Casting involves pouring liquid metal into a mold and then allowing it to cool and solidify. The solidified part is ejected or broken out of the mold to complete the process.

After working several months, Gorman had sculpted numerous clay models and took them to the foundry to make the molds. After the molds had been made, the bronze was melted in the furnace and poured into the molds. This successful collaboration between Gorman and the foundry produced eleven bronze statues.

In a touching ceremony on Veteran's Day in 1995, Gorman donated his father's bronze statue to Northern Arizona University in Flagstaff. Most of the remaining Code Talkers, dignitaries, and hundreds of Native American students attended the ceremony.

It was a glorious day for R.C. unlike the day three years ago, when he attended a ceremony for the five-hundredth anniversary of Columbus' sailing into the new world with his three small vessels, *Nina, Pinta* and *Santa Maria.*

Columbus Day has always been a day to celebrate Columbus as the hero who discovered America. But, during the years of the revolutionary digital age, there is a new perspective on the image of this legendary voyager. Since the traditional printed information has become an instant digital phenomenon, able to reach millions of readers instantly, especially the youth who most likely never read a newspaper, the Columbus historical image has been under question. Historians are now debating whether he was a hero or someone who caused much pain suffering to the Natives. Many stories have surfaced to questioned Columbus' reputation.

The bishop of Chiapas, Bartolome de la Casas, an historian and theologian, closely recounted the adventures of Columbus' four major voyages and provided a profound image that has done much damage to Columbus' reputation. La Casas' father and uncles sailed with Columbus, and he met the explorers as well. After witnessing the atrocities done to the Natives on the mainland and the islands, La Casas became a tireless defender of the Natives and crossed the Atlantic several times to bring awareness of his cause.

Before his monumental manuscript *History of the Indies,* written in the mid-fifteen hundreds and published in 1875, he published several shorter books recounting valuable information about Columbus and the Spanish colonial rules.

La Casas had been a tireless proponent of human rights. However, his opponents argued that he reshaped the truth, exaggerated about the loss of life and sometimes wrote about places he had never been. Nevertheless, his remarks about areas he never visited were drawn from official reports. Furthermore, some recent estimates of the population of that time in the places he wrote about, argue that the loss of life was higher than even Las Casas estimated.

La Casas' writings continue to be controversial, but he remains a major figure in the historical scholarship about human rights.

The writings of La Casas are long and his recounting of atrocities committed against the Natives are disturbing to the human soul. A much different version of Columbus and the colonists are portrayed by the American history textbooks. You decide who got it wrong.

The pinnacle of protesting the celebrated explorer was in 1992, the five-hundredth anniversary of Columbus discovering America. Protesters took the streets in the United States and around the world to voice their displeasure of idolizing a man who, in their opinion was a murdered and a slaver. In many cities, the parades were canceled and those who braved the threats and paraded regardless were under heavy police protection. Even though most Americans still think highly of the discoverer, the year of 1992 brought a much more realistic awareness to the general public about Columbus and the colonial rule.

Schools across the country were beginning to abandon the simplistic hero-only version of Columbus. Some states and cities canceled the parades and changed the name from Columbus Day to Indigenous People's Day.

It has been over five-hundred years since October of 1492 when Columbus braved the vast oceans and sailed his three tiny ships to discover America. Christopher Columbus never dreamed that five hundred years later people will portray him as a villain.

In the United States and around the world, especially in Latin America, on Columbus's five-hundredth anniversary, protests engaged in passionate and sometimes violent skirmishes against ceremonies honoring the famous explorer. The goal of the protesters was to depict Columbus as the catalyst of slaughter and environmental destruction that left the

American Natives with only a shred of their rightful heritage.

R.C. Gorman was a guest at a luncheon held in New York for the five-hundredth Columbus' anniversary. The guest of honor was a descendant of Columbus, the Duke of Veragua.

Gorman's appearance stirred an uproar by thousands of banner-waving and vocalizing protesters clustered outside around the entrance. They were angered to see R.C. clad in gold rings, bracelets and chains walking into the controversial event.

It wasn't one of Gorman's best days. In a later interview, he said that wearing the gold was a gesture to show the Duke that despite Columbus' atrocities, the Native Americans had survived and prospered. He reportedly told the Duke, pointing to his gold, that the Spanish came here for the this, but we still have it.

In a strange twist of fate, perhaps it was this event that propelled Gorman to start the bronze production and donate the statue to Northern Arizona University, to show solidarity with his tribe, by honoring the heroic deeds of the Navajo.

I spoke with one of Gorman's close friends and he admitted that Gorman was distraught by the protesters who misunderstood his gesture.

I was fortunate, when I moved to the Southwest, to be able to learn more and appreciate the Native American culture. Until then, my knowledge was from the movies I watched growing up in Europe which portrayed the Native Americans as savages. No wonder when we played Cowboys and Indians as children, everyone wanted to be a cowboy.

Maybe, my friend, you know the man with the box of sweets I met in Taos, was right comparing the Europeans with the Native Americans by respecting their culture.

Since the beginning of time, when conquerors began their search for new lands and the colonial empires oppressed the weak, there has been much looting of national treasures. The plundering of treasures has gone on for much too long and disregarded as not newsworthy until, in recent years, the rightful owners of many countries are demanding the return of their cultural treasures.

A few years ago, an auction house in Paris included sacred Native American objects. The controversial sale involved many Navajo ceremonial masks and despite the efforts by the U.S. Embassy and the Navajo Nation officials, the auction was to go on.

Ceremonial masks are sacred to Native Americans. When diplomacy and a plea to return sacred ceremonial masks failed, officials from the Navajo Nation traveled to the Paris auction intending to retrieve the masks and bring them home – at any cost. Fortunately, the Navajo representatives ended up bidding for the masks against an individual who backed down when he realized how important the masks were to the tribal members.

Despite Gorman's misstep on Columbus Day, intentional or not, he had always taken notes from history. The lessons he learned from his art heroes, Picasso and Dali, was that to be a superstar you must be the art; to live and breathe art, to create a persona and generate energy through your art.

At first, R.C. loved to do southwestern art, mainly surrealistic landscapes of the desert. There are some landscape paintings from his earlier career, but he stopped doing landscapes, claiming that he was out of his element. Gorman felt that he needed to create his own style; to be separated from the multitude of the "starving artists."

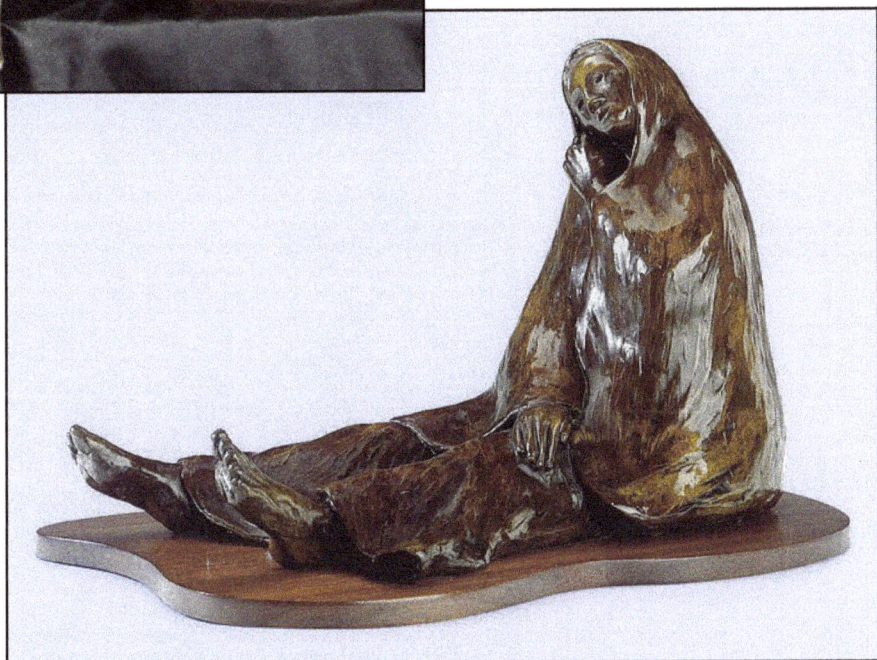

22

FISH OR PORK

During my trips to Taos, I spoke with many people and heard many stories about R.C. Gorman. There is no doubt that Gorman was the life of the party – any party. And he liked pets, unusual ones; most of them gifts from his friends. One of those gifts was a pet pig. It was given to him by a Houston doctor who frequently visited Gorman in Taos. To be exact, it was the doctor's girlfriend, a Gorman fan, who brought the doctor to Taos for the first time.

Nothing unusual about this story because many people traveled to Taos to meet Gorman until the story broke that the doctor was a married man and Taos had become his gateway place to spend time with his lover. Gorman and the doctor became good friends, and sometimes Gorman would tease him by saying - if you don't buy my art, I'll call your wife.

The doctor in return, not sure if it was intended as a joke, sent Gorman a pig pet on a leash, with a note, "thank you for keeping my secret". Gorman named the pig Corazon and let him loose in his studio. The pig must have been a dog in his past life because he would chase cars going through the narrow street of the gallery; he would run and bark, well, more accurately, oink loudly and grunt.

After several months Corazon mysteriously disappeared. Gorman and friends searched the area, but Corazon was not to be found.

It was at this time that Gorman discovered one of his bookkeepers was embezzling money from his business. Apparently, he had been getting away with it for a while. He was creating false invoices and charged personal expenses to the business. The bookkeeper was fired. A few weeks later, the bookkeeper had a big party in a restaurant. Gorman was invited, and not knowing how to say no to any party, of course, he went – it was put together with his money after all.

The party was great; there was much drinking and a lot of food, including roasted pork. Despite the ill feelings about the bookkeeper who stole his money, Gorman had a great time until when he was about to leave. All of the sudden he had a strange feeling that he ate his pet pig. He glanced at the bookkeeper with a horrified look; the bookkeeper smiled back - a mysterious smile.

Gorman was speechless and furious. Not knowing what to do, he slowly headed back to his studio vowing to never eat pork again.

Lee Archuleta was waiting by his studio door. Gorman first met this boy outside a bar, where Gorman was to deliver a painting. In the bar, the buyer was trying to bargain the price. Gorman insisted that the price was two thousand dollars. The buyer tried to bargain the price down to one thousand dollars. After a few bargaining exchanges without reaching an agreement, and several drinks later, Gorman ripped the painting in half and handed the half to the buyer, saying – "Here is the half of it for a thousand dollars when you pay the rest I will give you the other half."

Gorman stormed out of the bar and there, outside the door was Lee, trying to sell him some chili. He told Gorman that he waited outside for him because he was too young to go into the bar. They quickly became friends and, eventually, Lee's parents, too poor to raise the boy, asked Gorman to become Lee's guardian. Gorman accepted the task and made sure that the boy went to school. Lee grew up around Gorman, traveled with him and finally settled in Taos. Lee fell in love, married and he and his wife took care of Gorman's plants and garden and did routine maintenance on the house.

One of the people I was introduced to was Roy, who moved to Taos in 1979 and was considered by some to be very knowledgeable about the town's history. He was also a good friend of Gorman. "When I first moved to Taos, I used to go to Mr. Gorman's gallery. He always dropped what he was doing to help me. He was a smart businessman and taught me a lot about the business, and I wasn't the only one. He helped many people succeed. His philosophy was that the more successful galleries, the more people would come to Taos. I and many others owe Gorman everything we have accomplished."

In my questioning about Gorman, the businessman, he responded,

"He was a marketing genius. He ran incredible radio adds, and when he was signing autographs, he would turn on his charm. He created a one-of-a-kind persona, difficult to forget, with his headband and Hawaiian shirts. I remember when he was on Good Morning America with Joan Lunden. We all woke early in the morning to watch him. You know there were no recordings back then; you had to watch everything live. He was funny and straightforward on that show. Soon after, Taos witnessed increase traffic into the city."

He continued,

"In 1982, he jump-started the Taos Celebration of Arts and it is still going on. It is a spectacular celebration to start the busy season, with exhibits, music, poetry, and art. I remember Governor Richardson came to town to speak, and when he asked, 'Does anyone have ideas to promote the city, I am listening.' I spoke up and said that the state should do a national promotion for the arts. He proposed that if we raised thirty thousand dollars, the state would match the funds. I went to Gorman and asked his help to raise the money. He raised the money in a couple of months by selling autographed Gorman images!"

When asked about what made Gorman so successful, other than his talent and charm, he answered, "The people he surrounded himself with, especially Virginia and Rose. Virginia was very loyal and protective of him. She guarded him from people who were trying to take advantage of his fame. And Rose had everything ready for him and for his parties in the house. Without them, he would not have been able to function as well as he did."

He remembered once when he visited his gallery; he asked Gorman if he was tired of doing the same thing. Gorman surprised him by showing him a series of incredible abstract paintings and nudes.

"I don't do the same thing. But this is what the publishers want to sell. They don't want the nudes. What am I supposed to do with these?"

"Why don't you do something different with the nudes, like a cookbook" Roy suggested.

The seed was planted for his *Nudes and Foods* cookbook and Gorman began to collect recipes from friends and with the collaboration of Virginia and Rose, the book was soon published.

"In a couple of words how you characterize Gorman's presence in Taos?"

"Huge. Entertaining. Gorman was Taos."

When asked if he met any of the celebrities that used to flock to Taos during the Gorman era.

"Yes. There was quite a lineup visiting here. Liz Taylor actually bought a piece from my gallery. She was kind and sweet."

Roy went on to say that the general belief was that Elizabeth Taylor went to Taos to meet Gorman. That is false. She used to visit Taos to see her brother, but she and Gorman eventually became good friends.

Howard Taylor moved to Taos after several failing attempts to become a movie star and a few unsuccessful business ventures. In Taos, he dropped out of public life. The only time he surfaced in public was when he opened an art gallery in Taos. His gallery eventually failed and he went back to living a reclusive life.

"Liz Taylor tried to convince Gorman to quit drinking," Roy commented.

"What about his drinking habits? Did that affect his work?" I asked.

"I don't think so. He was up in the morning worked for about six hours and then went into town to have lunch and drink lots of wine."

Roy said that often Gorman would call him to have lunch with him.

His staff would tell him not to come back after a lunch with Gorman. Having lunch with Gorman was a long affair. Before talking to the chefs about food, a bottle or two of wine would be gone between him and his guests. During and after lunch there would be more wine.

"Gorman was well read with a great sense of humor and often he would laugh at himself."

"What would you remember from those times?"

"The legendary dinners in his house. The great parties. People rejoicing, hanging around his swimming pool. Gorman was always reaching for the stars. He bought the best and ate the best. He enjoyed life to the fullest. At the same time, many people made a lot of money because of him."

"Do you miss him?"

"Yes. Very much. Taos is not the same without Gorman. It was a glorious time while he was around."

The sound of his voice choked with emotions, remembering celebrated times of the past.

Everyone in Gorman's home was overcome with excitement when Jackie Kennedy was coming to spend the day and have lunch with R.C.

After talking art with Gorman for a while, Jackie went to the kitchen to help Rose prepare lunch. The two seemed to be having a great time chopping, cooking, and talking foods.

After a lengthy lunch, Jackie thanked everyone and promised to return. When Gorman was asked about Jackie working in the kitchen, his answer was "She is Jackie Kennedy, she can do anything she wants and I am okay with that." He also said in an interview that Rose told him that when Jackie came to Taos, it went a few levels up in class. The lunch menu with Jackie included salads, meat and fish.

Fish? I thought the Navajo people do not eat fish!

Traditionally, the Navajos will not eat fish. Partly because of religious beliefs and partly because they live in a desert and there's not that many fish around to eat. Therefore, they have not cultivated a taste for it.

During World War II, someone tried to sell fish to the Navajos. It was when most of the men were away at war and the women were raising children, herding sheep, farming, keeping the family together and waiting for the men to return.

During this time, a peculiar man showed up in the Chinle area. He had a heavy German accent and offered to sell shrimp and fish to the Navajos. The man kept showing up, trying to sell fish and asking curious questions. Eventually, the women figured out that this man was a spy trying to get information about the code talkers, and everyone stopped talking to him.

I mean, come on. What were the Germans thinking by sending the worst spy agent they had, trying to sell fish to the Navajos!

Eventually, Gorman started to eat fish, especially after he gave up eating pork.

Remember the guy who was bargaining with Gorman about the painting he finally ripped in half? He had moved to California. More than ten years after Gorman's death, he walked into the Scottsdale's R.C. Gorman Navajo Gallery holding his half of the painting, looking for the other half.

23

GOING HOLLYWOOD

The sixties was a decade of prosperity and protest, and during those turbulent times of social unrest, the United States forever changed. The first steps of a groundbreaking movement to end the rule of superiority, dominated mostly by white males who believed that any other gender or race was an inferior minority, was gaining momentum. The voices of the few courageous individuals began to creep into in the social conscience and pave the way for acceptance that all humans are equal. It was a time that some individuals in the entertaining field, unafraid of the consequences for their careers, initiated the long rocky road to restoring the image of the Native Americans. Two of the most vocal proponents of Native American causes were the very best of their industries.

One of the most powerful moments in Hollywood history was when Marlon Brando, considered by many critics to be the best actor ever, refused to accept the movie industry's highest honor, for his gut-wrenching performance in *The Godfather*.

Brando was protesting the fact that the Native Americans were portrayed in films as savage, hostile, and evil. He was concerned about children growing up in such world, especially the Native American children; their minds injured seeing their race depicted in such a negative light. Brando, having eighty-five-million viewers, used this rare opportunity for political justice. To refuse the Oscar was a small price to pay to raise awareness about the struggles of the Native American communities.

Another celebrity who risked his career to bring awareness of the Native American struggles was the one-and-only Johnny Cash. It was at the height of his career when he recorded *Bitter Tears*, an album in support of Native American rights. The controversial lyrics of the song, *As Long As The Grass Shall Grow*, caused an uproar of protests and threats about ending his career.

We are talking about Johnny Cash here, a tenacious man, unafraid of controversy. He fought back against the industry's elite, who wanted to boycott against his voice, by producing another controversial single, *The Ballad of Ira Hayes*, a Pima Indian who helped raise the flag on Iwo Jima, then died an alcoholic at a very young age.

Cash then took out full page ads in various magazines in protest, calling for disk jockeys, station managers, radio owners, and music studios executives, to grow-up and pay attention to racial tension, the struggles, and the wars that were beginning to tear apart the nation. His acts gave a huge boost to tribal rights.

It was the action of the pioneer activists of human rights that paved the way for Native American artists and entertainers to find the spotlight, through their talent.

I believe that artists like R.C. Gorman were the benefactors of the courageous individuals who used their spotlight to promote worthy social agendas. It was partly because of the groundbreaking social movement of the sixties that paved the road to Taos for R.C. Gorman. For over twenty-five years, Taos was once again one of the main destinations for art lovers and the principal attraction was the name of R.C. Gorman. It was during these prosperous years that R.C. gained fame, and along with him, many others gained wealth, creating an affluent community in Taos, and a comfortable life for the entire community.

The voguish Gorman movement did not escape Hollywood.

Soap opera stars like Jeanne Cooper, Terry Lester, David Marx, were some of the earliest stars to trek up on the path to find R.C. Gorman's Navajo Gallery. During the visits of the soap opera stars, Gorman involved the Taos people by inviting several ladies into his house to meet and talk with their favorite stars.

Maria Shriver visited Taos often to see Gorman's new works. Eventually, she brought along Arnold Schwarzenegger. We think of Arnold as a tough man that single-handedly kills the inhabitants of an entire city, but he showed his sensitivity when it came to Gorman's work. After his first visit, he told Gorman, "I'll be back." And he did, and brought along his buddy Danny DeVito. Schwarzenegger has a collection of over thirty of Gorman's original pieces. Arnold and DeVito loved to hang out with Gorman, smoking cigars and drinking screwdrivers.

Gorman again wanted to share the Terminator's popularity with the people of Taos. He invited the Taos High School wrestling team and bodybuilders to his home to meet Arnold. The young men took pictures with the Terminator and went home with autographed photos and stories to tell.

There is a picture of Arnold with Gorman. On the picture Arnold wrote: "Of course, with R.C.'s body and my artistic talents we could conquer the world."

Rose, Gorman's housekeeper, loved Danny DeVito. She thought he was the funniest person alive and the fact that he loved her cooking and always told her so, warmed her heart.

By the time Elizabeth Taylor received her third Academy Award, she and R.C. Gorman had become great friends. Gorman told her since she already had two Oscars why not give the third one to him. They both had a good laugh and of course that did not happen, but Ms. Taylor surprised Gorman with a glass statuette replica of the third Oscar made for him and presented it to him on one of the parties at his home. Elizabeth Taylor and Dennis Hopper, who was a resident of Taos and another one of Gorman's friend, crossed paths often during Gorman's parties. Of course, they knew each other from acting together in the movie *Giant*, also starring Rock Hudson and James Dean. The movie earned ten Academy awards. It was

James Dean's last movie.

It is well known that Elizabeth Taylor loved diamonds. She wore them with anything and she loved to party, especially when around Gorman. There was a time when R.C., after having a little too much to drink, gave her a fashion lecture, telling her that "It takes a lot of nerve to mix turquoise with diamonds."

Taos was becoming a second Hollywood with the ongoing parade of stars. Gorman delivered his art to Gregory Peck's house, an avid art collector. He tried to compete in fast talking with Cloris Leachman. He was hanging out with Ray Conniff, Burt Reynolds and trying to animate a shy Peter Fonda. He had dinner with Caesar Romero and Erma Bombeck, with sports celebrities like golf legend Arnold Palmer and pitcher Jim Palmer and politicians, among them Senator Barry Goldwater and governor Bill Richardson.

He would play piano with Sandy Duncan, while Rose was missing Danny DeVito and often asking when was he coming back. Gorman and his staff welcomed President Jimmy Carter and the first lady Rosalyn Carter, Lee Marvin, Arlo Guthrie and Shirley MacLaine.

And the list goes on and on.

Besides the many entertainer friends, Gorman had many artist friends , one of his closest friend was Andy Warhol.

24

THE ODD COUPLES

In Arizona, there is a richness of natural beauty and endless possibilities of outdoor adventures. One of the most beautiful places is the unique area of Sedona. It is where thousands of Phoenicians flock during summertime to escape the scorching heat of the Phoenix valley.

Oak Creek is next to Sedona along Highway 89A, a scenic route twisting its way through Oak Creek Canyon all the way to Flagstaff. This route is one of the most beautiful drives anywhere. Towering trees lined along the breathless rock formations of the canyon's narrow walls with natural water springs winding below. Moving further north towards Flagstaff, the foliage of the pine forests creates spectacular scenery along the dramatic rock formations and the changing colors of its cliffs. There are many fun-filled family activities in this area including several amazing hiking trails.

It was during a family getaway to Oak Creek that I had the opportunity to visit the R.C. Gorman Navajo gallery in Sedona.

The two clerks attending were very helpful in explaining about R.C. Gorman's work. However, once they realized the extent of knowledge about Gorman's life and art, I had to confess that I was writing a book about his life.

The female clerk smiled and said "about time" and went on to ask questions about his life's journey.

After a conversation about the progression of his art throughout the decades she confessed to being a long-time fan of Gorman since she lived in Mexico in the seventies, "It is the reason I am working here" she said, "to be around his art."

She continued to say that from all his work, she loved the older pieces and took me on tour to show me her favorite ones.

She pointed out the true-hearted expressions of both *Era* and *Pablita*. "I love the expressions on both. It is like looking in a mirror," she said. Then she showed me the *Gambling Lady*, a woman with a mysterious smile, holding the ace of spades. I am not sure the significance of that since Gorman was not a gambler. Maybe it was reminiscent of the time he was a boy watching his father gamble. All the images she pointed out were done in the late Seventies.

"What is it that you like about Gorman's work?" I asked.

"His treatment of women. How he portrays women's habits, strength, and knowledge. He would sometimes treat them quietly, sometimes with immense personality and power, but always with dignified realism. It is fair to assume that women had a strong influence in his life."

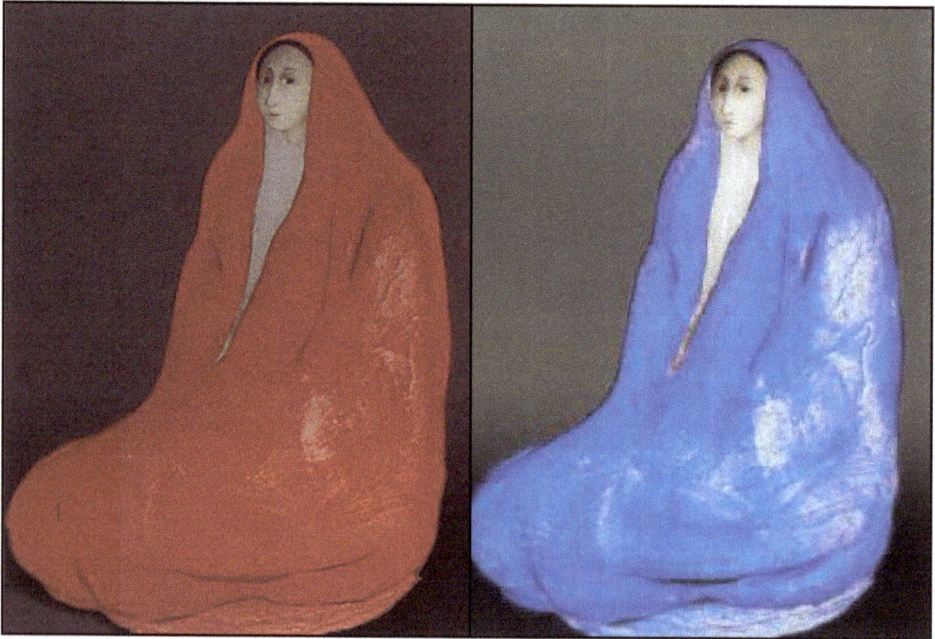

Era I   *Era II*

Pablita

Gambling Lady

The man working in the gallery was interested in Gorman's time with Fritz Scholder. I was thankful that he reminded me about Scholder because it would be neglectful not to mention Scholder's immense contribution to the Native American arts. Although Scholder was part

Native American, one-third Luiseno, a small tribe living near Oceanside in California, he became one of the most renowned Native American artists of the twentieth century.

In the history of arts and theater, there were several odd couples who were friends or worked together who gave us laughs and memorable moments. Such friends were Laurel and Hardy, Twain and Tesla, Richie and The Fonz, Mozart and Haydn, Felix and Oscar and DeVito with Arnold, to name a few.

Gorman and Scholder were also an odd couple. They connected in the early Seventies, in the Tamarind Institute shortly after Tamarind moved from Los Angeles to the New Mexico's College of Fine Arts.

They did just one exhibition together in the Museum of New Mexico in Santa Fe. The two styles were very different, but their work had a great influence on how the world outside the reservation perceived the Native Americans. Scholder's multicultural background reflected in his work as he attempted to merge Native Americans with American pop culture. He painted Native Americans wrapped in the American flag and holding a beer can or wearing a buffalo headdress holding an ice cream cone.

His work was controversial, but Scholder was immune to criticism, whether people loved or hated his paintings. He was more interested in people experiencing some kind of a reaction.

Gorman was concerned about the beauty and strength of the Native Americans while Scholder was interested in their problems.

Even though they were at odds in their antithetical approach of the Native American principle, they remained good friends.

Andy Warhol was the leading artist of the sixties Pop Art movement, an elusive form of art that escaped the conventional fine art and mainstream aesthetics. Warhol, with his uniquely whimsical style, ventured into an art that was both controversial and imaginative. His creativeness paved a new direction for artists to follow. Whatever variety of art forms he introduced became immediately trendy. Besides soup cans, coca cola bottles, shoes, cars, vacuum cleaners and hamburgers, he painted celebrity portraits. His most famous subjects among many were Marilyn Monroe, Jackie Kennedy, Elizabeth Taylor, Mick Jagger, John Lennon and Mohamed Ali; works that earned him a fortune. However, the one that became one of the most valuable paintings in history was the *Eight Elvises* which sold in 2008 for $100 million. Warhol's life was blessed with success and marked with misfortunes, particularly in 1968 when his career almost ended. He was shot by Valerie Solanas, an aspiring writer who was reportedly upset with Warhol for refusing to use a script she had written. Warhol was seriously wounded in this attack and spent a few weeks in a New York hospital.

Warhol died at the young age of fifty-eight, on February of 1987 from sudden cardiac arrest, following an operation to remove his gallbladder.

Warhol's extremely quiet, enigmatic personality seemed to get along with Gorman's enormous energetic, flamboyant style. The fact that they became good friends is one of those mysteries that drives a writer insane to find the reasons why.

But when those two appeared together in public, it was a major attraction.

Imagine the Beatles and Rolling Stones on the same stage or Jordan and Magic on the same team – like that.

Warhol and Gorman, besides being good friends, collected each-other's work and also painted one another. Their only exhibit together in 1978 caused a major traffic jam in the streets of New York.

Gorman was invited to a dinner in Washington hosted by Vice President Walter Mondale and his wife Joan, in honor of the American Contemporary Artist. Gorman was seated at Joan Mondale's right side and Andy Warhol was seated on her left.

The right ear of Mrs. Mondale was buzzing from Gorman's talk and laughter while there was quietness on her left since Warhol remained soundless.

Gorman had tremendous respect for Warhol and defended him when critics put him down, saying that those who do not understand art should tone down the criticism of a great artist such as Warhol. Personally, though he would often joke with Warhol telling him that he looked like a rag-doll and tried to give him fashion tips but Warhol would answer that he was an original so was his look. When out to dinner, Gorman would say that it feels strange just to sit there and have Warhol watch him eat while he was not eating anything. But that was Warhol; quiet and strange versus Gorman animated and talkative.

Gorman's art has brought joy to a vast number of art lovers. Through lithography and giclee prints, tens of thousands of people have been able to marvel at the composed, indomitable image of the Native American woman. Gorman's personification of gracefulness and strength of the female form, those he called *My Madonnas,* is unmatched.

Other than the conventional Madonna-types illustrated on religious icons, very few were able to capture the woman's form when composed with a persuasive attitude. On the contrary, some have seriously failed, like Parmigiano's *The Madonna With The Long Neck.* Unlike the calm and peaceful Madonna of his master Raphael, Parmigianino's is a curious composition, starting with the giraffe-like neck. His work exhibits an almost supernatural creature with abnormal human proportions. Not sure if that was his idea of portraying the ideal woman's beauty or trying to make some statement, but whatever he was trying to do ended up as a confusing image, especially the oversize Christ child that unfolds across Madonna's lap.

Scholder, Gorman and Warhol left behind their mark in the art world. But most important, they originated a direction to inspire many individuals of unconventional backgrounds, spontaneous personalities or with controversial ideas, to step forward and announce their presence. And, to be an example of endurance; despite being subjects of resentful character attacks by some, they never abandoned their dreams.

I get it when people are critiquing a piece of art – even great artists sometimes create unpleasant images. But to continuously attack an artist for his or her personality, lifestyle, and looks, like some people kept doing to the artists above, goes beyond civilized human behavior.

The need to feel important by demeaning someone's character for no reason exposes the insecurity of an individual.

Thinking about one's ambiguity, I was reminded of a famous Jamaican proverb: *"Those who can't dance blame it on the music."* Then, for some strange reason, the lyrics of the *"Bohemian Rhapsody"* by Queen crept into my head: *"Scaramouche, Scaramouche, can you do the fandango?"*

25

MIND AND BODY

There was a gentle falling snow in the evening when Rose Roybal and her friend Shirley walked into the warmness of the Navajo Gallery. A few people were strolling around; some were drinking wine, others gathered in small groups talking and laughing. This place wasn't the stereotypical art gallery - someone to welcome people at the door, quiet whispers covered a soft music while people moved slowly looking at the art.

In the Navajo Gallery, the person that welcomed the two ladies was the one-and-only R.C. Gorman. He walked up to them, "Welcome, welcome friends," he shouted with his arms wide open beaming a broad smile. R.C. told them to feel free to look around and ask questions, "but don't leave without buying something," his laughter thundered across the room. Virginia approached the two friends; she shook her head smiling, offering the guests wine and appetizers and saying, "Don't mind R.C., he is always saying things like that." Shirley knew R.C. well, but Rose only knew him by reputation. The two friends spoke with R.C. many times throughout the evening about food and art and Rose learned that Gorman was moving to Las Colonias, near her house. The two ladies had stopped in the gallery for a short visit, but by the time they left, it was past midnight. After meeting R.C., Rose could not stop thinking about him.

Shortly after her visit to the gallery, Rose went out of town for a month. Upon her return home, she received a phone call from someone who claimed to be R.C. Gorman. At first, she thought that this was a joke, but after the person on the other end of the line had told her about meeting her over a month ago, Rose realized that it was Gorman himself. She was speechless for a moment. The next word that came out of her mouth was, "Yes." This was after Gorman asked her if she wanted to work for him, to be his housekeeper and help him in his kitchen.

It was a phone call that changed her life.

Rose began working for Gorman in the late seventies, a time when Taos was the place to be for art lovers. She was there to help when Gorman moved to his big house in Las Colonias. At first, she started as a cleaning lady, soon after she became his cook and housekeeper. Rose Roybal was a frequent travel companion of R.C. both within the United States and abroad.

She met Hollywood celebrities and well-known politicians, planned hundreds of parties, prepared endless meals and accompanied R.C. in famous restaurants around the world. She even helped R.C. to write a cookbook. She herself became a celebrity.

A long time has passed since those days of youth.

For Gorman, there was a period of a deep depression after Rose died of a brain tumor in 2002. A few years before Rose died, his father passed, leaving a big void in his life. But, without Rose, there was an inexplicable emptiness in his house and his life.

His public appearances were limited to important dinner gatherings and close friends' outings. Gorman was now walking with the help of a dark polished wooden cane with a silver handle. Even though his mind was shadowed by sadness, he was trying to maintain his spirited self when in public.

Normally, the body knows when it is time to slow down but in Gorman's case, his mind remained determined; he thought he could handle another party, another dance, another bottle of wine, and he tried to, despite the resistance from the body.

Usually, in large dinner parties, he tried to reflect on the days of youth.

Gorman was at a dinner party about a year before he became seriously ill. He was standing up telling his stories, wine glass in one hand, cane for support in the other hand. He was laughing and lightening up the mood in the room, and veering the entire room toward party mode. Gorman was telling an animated story with a passionate voice, waving his cane around to emphasize his point. Everyone stood up and clapped. It was a moment of passion and self-indulgence.

The guests at the long table, twenty or so of them, raised their wine glasses among the cheers and laughter. Gorman spoke, guests laughed, glasses raised to a salute, emptied, and raised once again. His cane waved faster as his story was coming to an end. Everyone was looking at him. The sound waves of the laughter and the loud voices bouncing off the walls created a raucous atmosphere. Suddenly, there was an awful noise; Gorman's body slammed on the floor, sounds of glasses breaking, the cane sliding across the floor, the boisterous noises were reduced to concern whispers. The guests scrambled to help Gorman up. For several minutes before the fall, Gorman's body was trying to tell him to sit down, but his mind wouldn't listen and the inevitable did happen; he crashed - face first on the floor. There were quiet voices as people were trying to help him back on his feet. The only loud sound was Gorman's laugh, "I am fine, I am fine."

How are you fine R.C.? You are laying on pieces of broken glass with a lake of Merlot around you.

He was lifted off the floor, "Please, please have fun, don't worry about me."

One of his favorite things to say was, "Enjoy life – you only live once."

Yes. But. R.C. you only have two legs and both are bad.

Often, when in town and having had a bit too much to drink, there was someone who would help him, either getting him home or taking his keys away and calling a friend. The city people protected him. He was still R.C. Gorman.

Eventually, he realized that he had to obey his body and was quick to admit that he was mellowing out, especially after knee surgeries and a knee replacement and later on, surgery for a subdural hematoma that kept him confined to his home for a few months.

Besides his cane, he also used an electric scooter to get around. He seemed to be coping well, signing hundreds of posters at his annual gallery show. But, life was certainly different from a few years ago when he used to live a Dionysian lifestyle.

At home, he still had Virginia and his family to keep him company, but he missed Rose's voice, sometimes calling him R.C., other times she called him Gorman, like when a mother calls the child's full name until she has his attention before she speaks.

One of Gorman's favorite pastimes now was to sit by his large window and look at his Taos mountains. He was known to say that he felt like a coyote. Those who were not Navajo or did not know the Navajo mythology were surprised to hear that Gorman compared himself to a coyote, an animal perceived as a hostile one. But Gorman knew what he was talking about. He sought the deeper spiritual meaning of that animal in himself.

The coyote is an indispensable symbol to the Navajo, one that portrays many facets of Navajo existence.

In the Navajo mythology, the Coyote is an unrestrained troublemaker but also one of the most revered and contradictory characters. In some myths he appears greedy and crafty, in some stories amusing and other times fearsome and proud. Gorman smiled as he remembered some of his friends telling him that he was a necessary pain in the neck - just like the coyote.

He was still a bigger-than-life figure in Taos. It wasn't only his overabundance of talent but also his great generosity.

At his annual event, all Taos galleries followed his lead, and a full docket of shows opens on the three-day event. There were traffic jams on the road between Santa Fe and Taos coming and going to his annual event, but for most of the visitors the inconvenience was worth it.

Among the thousands who came out to celebrate one of his last annual shows, was a friend who was struggling to raise his family. Gorman gave him one of his original drawings and asked his friend to sell it and use the money to take care his family. This gesture was one of the many he did to help others, one of many that he never bragged about.

Even though his legs were betraying him, his desire to run and dance and laugh remained hidden in him. It was this optimistic attitude, along with his natural and striking talent, which allowed him to rise out of the Navajo reservation and become one of the most influential and fascinating artists of his time.

Gorman was able to turn his brilliance into a hot commodity. The amazing thing is that he did it without compromising his place in the history of art. But his journey wasn't without adversities. I found one of his works that I thought might represent his feelings at the time.

His *Thunderstorm* was created in the late eighties. It was a time when he reached the height of his popularity and productivity. At that time, there were endless hours of work to keep up with the demand for his art but also there were the necessary social outings, especially with the Hollywood bunch. It is safe to acknowledge that along with his heavy working schedule, there was an increase of alcohol consumption.

His creation *Thunderstorm* is an image of three women, sitting calmly on the red earth watching a thick lavender color cloud that stretches across the sky touching the earth. Confined in this gentle cloud, there are forks of lightning threatening to burst out. Otherwise, the rest of the sky is soft blue with some soft pinkish clouds.

Often, I wondered what was he thinking when he created *Thunderstorm*. However, since getting into Gorman's head is nearly impossible; my best explanation was that he was trying to maintain order in his life before bursting out of control.

The color of the cloud in *Thunderstorm* is a sacred color to Native Americans; it is a symbolism of power and mystery. We know that the thunderstorm is a signal of disruption. The color red has different meanings; in a time of war, it represents blood and violence but in a time of celebration, it means beauty and happiness.

To me, this image represents his struggle to free himself from the pressing obligations and find a balance and harmony.

Even so, this is my best guess, one thing is a certainty about R. C. Gorman - he was unpredictable. You could never predict what he would do or say.

When the guests were leaving his gallery, Gorman usually would say, "Thank you for your money." Seriously, who says that to a customer! And he would laugh that deep contagious laughter of his.

To everyone, he seemed to be the happiest creature in the world. Only, he knew full well that there was a narrow passage between laughter and pain.

Thunderstorm

26

THE LAST DANCE

The Navajo healing ceremonies are a connection between the divine and the everyday survival. Their healing ceremonial performances use dancing and chanting as their focal points. The art of sand-painting is also used to cure specific ailments.

Navajo sand-painting is the elaborate art of pouring colored sands and other colored minerals to create temporary paintings for the healing ceremonies. It wasn't until the fifties when Navajo artists began to create permanent sand-painting images by arranging colored sand on glue-covered surfaces.

There are many additional activities like face-paintings, pollen blessings, and prayer chants, as well gambling, horse racing, great feasts, clowns, poetry, and various fun games. The ceremonial healing events are also part of the community gatherings, to renew their tribal commonality.

Rudy, as did every Navajo child, grew up on the heartfelt prayers, sacred songs and spectacular dances performed during these long, somber rituals.

What is most likely the biggest ceremony of the year is the Mountain Chant, a nine-day event that takes place at the end of winter and marks a transition in the seasons.

The Fire Dance that concludes the ceremony just before dawn of the ninth night is the eleventh dance of the night.

During the night, young men feed the central fire with wood. As the fire crackles and intensifies, the tongues of flames become huge waves of fire, roaring towards the skies.

The dancing men, race in a circle around the fire and close to the unbearable heat, sweating, chanting louder and louder at the evil spirits.

Deeper into the night more dancers rush in and the intensity of the fire-dancers grows while the heat is still raging. Their cry is a sound made with their tongue against their lips, like the fluttering of a rapidly burning fire. The night seems to last a long time until the last fire spark subside. At this time, the medicine man walks around the subdued fire sprinkling meal and pollen and chanting prayers of sanctification.

By sunrise all ceremonies are completed, the fire is reduced to ashes and the darkness is replaced with the light.

For the Navajo, this ceremony's purpose is to purify and remove all ugly things from their lives.

Besides sweating around the fire, purification occurs from consuming herbal medicine and ritual bathing.

Fire Dancer

The Mountain Chant ceremony chronicles the legendary adventures of the young hero Dsilyi Neyani, the lost son of a Navajo family. He was on a hunting trip and was captured by the Navajo enemy, the Utes. He eventually escaped with the help of the gods. His journey to get back to his people was full of enormous undertakings, like the Odyssey but instead took place in mountains, caves, and forests rather than the sea and islands.

During his adventures, he was taught healing, magic, sand-painting and how to performs various ceremonial deeds. Once he proved himself worthy, his body and soul were transformed into a heroic image by the deities.

On his attempt to fly away from the enemy, the Utes pursued to try and recapture him. Dsilyi Neyani at first had to pass over an area of fallen trees and huge rocks that were blocking his way through a canyon. A soft white cloud was sent to him by the gods to help him through, but the cloud was so soft he could not step on it, so the gods sent him a white rainbow that spanned the canyon and he used it as a bridge to cross onto the other side.

Across the canyon, the young man entered a cave through a small hole in the mountain cliff. There he found clothes so he could be dressed properly for his journey. He was kept warm by a burning fire that was surrounded by four colored paddles to guide his direction; black to the east, blue to the south, yellow to the west, and white to the north.

The Utes had lost his trail temporarily.

Leaving the first cave, he passed volcanic rocks, met various animals, including a black sheep, and four bears, colored black, blue, yellow, and white to point him in the right direction. The young hero passed through mountain peaks and forests of pine and spruce. He braved thunder, hail storms and violent winds.

Along the way, the gods named him Dsilyi Neyani and this is how he was known among his people.

The wind-god helped Dsilyi Neyani through a passage guarded by two angry rattlesnakes. Beyond the passage, there was a forest of piñon trees. Under the trees, the gods taught him the art of Shamanism.

The Utes appeared again, pursuing him.

The young hero found refuge in the house of butterflies, a dwelling house full of rainbows where he was given a bath by the *Butterfly Woman* in a basin made by a large white shell.

The *Butterfly Woman* told him that before meeting his people, he had to be proper and clean. Then she applied fine cornmeal to his feet and in all parts of his wounds for healing. The *Feather Woman* painted his face and body and asked him to dance around the fire. After the dance, the *Butterfly Woman* pulled his hair back and made it long, down past his waist and pressed his body and face until he was molded into a beautiful young man, all the while a flock of colorful butterflies hovered around the room. Then the women pointed in a direction towards a wooded mountain and asked him to follow the trail to that mountain. It was at that mountain that he met the *Holy Woman*, she led him to the four colored trees, black, blue, yellow, and white, to guide the young hero toward his way home. The *Butterfly Woman* distracted the Utes so that Dsilyi Neyani's could go up to the wooden mountain. Along with the wind-god, she helped the young hero pass through several other houses, including the house of cherries, where he met a supernatural young woman who pointed out four large logs painted in the four colors of the four cardinal directions.

Along the way home, he met the Navajo shaman who helped the young hero build a medicine lodge and collect plants for the new rights and the purification ceremonies. The ceremonies performed by the shaman cured Dsilyi Bryant of all of his strange feelings and notions.

The butterfly is very important to the Navajo

It is in her home that the young hero was cured of all wounds and transformed into a strong, beautiful young man.

R. C. Gorman acknowledged the significance of the butterfly in several of his images, all later in his life. First was with the *Monarch* in 1993. There was another one called *Stella De Oro* in 1995, a Navajo woman watching a giant monarch butterfly on a large sunflower plant. And two more, *Mariposa* and *Mariposa II* just before his passing in 2005.

Monarch

Stella De Oro

It has been over seventy years since Rudy witness the sand-paintings done by his forefathers and was mesmerized for the first time with fire, songs and dances. R.C. Gorman lived a full life, one of ongoing celebrations and with an ardent passion for living life to the fullest, always in dancing style, walking with a swagger and feeling successful, even when he wasn't making money. Gorman's best asset was not only his ability to create incredible art but believing in himself – to never give up on his dream.

His biggest joy was to be recognized for his work, seeing people flock into his events. Like that time in Los Angeles that he was stuck in traffic and was late for his showing. When he arrived, he apologized for being late, "I was caught in that heavy terrific," he said.

"The heavy traffic is caused by the people who are coming to see you," was the answer from the gallery's director.

Gorman had a genuine mystique about him. With those quick flashes of personality, he could be as spontaneous as his drawing. When he was plagued by severe diabetes, he knew that his last dance was approaching. From his hospital bed he was relieved when he saw the new dawn and sunset because he was thinking that they might be the last ones.

It is difficult to leave behind the life you enjoy so much.

The end was near when he contracted a virulent blood infection.

On September 18, 2005, Gorman fell at his home and was taken to Holy Cross Hospital in Taos. A week later he was transferred to University Hospital in Albuquerque. From there he was taken back to his home to be laid to rest.

Rudy, the young boy, born in poverty who rose to be R.C. Gorman, one the most influential people of his time – this is the story here. In my quest to have a fair image of Gorman's character I had to examine his life by recounting a story of another fascinated character. A story that will convey the message that we should not judge someone from the last year or two on earth, when facing pain and the possibility of death but to reflect on their entire life.

Interpreting someone's life is a great responsibility. The words which the pen leaves behind are unforgiving; they could devastate or elevate people's emotions. I thought long and hard before choosing to paraphrase my most beloved tragic poet, Sophocles, and his masterpiece of King Oedipus of Thebes.

Sophocles perceived human grief as very few writers have ever done. He seems to be speaking the language of every generation - as Gorman's paintings do.

I believe that Sophocles, through his verse, was able to eliminate man's dark perplexities and could confront mysterious subjects with clarity. His ability to grant tenderness and nobility to the most hateful individual is unquestionable. Sophocles' restraint was his poetry's best quality.

Oedipus, the perplexed ruler, looked back at his city and questioned who caused such destruction to his city. Then he had an epiphany and cried out, "My god it was me. It was me!"

There are ongoing debates about Oedipus being an altruistic or egoistic ruler, mostly based on that moment.

I like to imagine a similar thought when Gorman was lying in his hospital bed, a moment of self-examination, looking at his beloved city and exclaiming, "Look what I have done for this city."

Sophocles' play of Oedipus, written in 429 BC pretty much summons my thoughts about the debate of Gorman's character.

Was R.C. Gorman altruistic or egoistic?

Was Oedipus a tyrant or a just ruler?

There was much talk about Gorman's eccentricity.

We already established that Gorman had a healthy dose of eccentricity.

I think that the definition of a person being eccentric is often misunderstood. The word *ekkentros,* was first used by the ancient Greek scientists to describe orbits of planets that were slightly out of whack. Eventually, it came to describe people who were unconventional, peculiar, and even interesting. Being eccentric, curious, idiosyncratic, unconventional, or whatever name we are willing to tag a person with, it is not a bad thing. I do not find this confusing at all.

However, what is confusing is the appropriate definition of altruism versus egoism. We must gain wealth before giving it back to help others. Therefore, we are using our egoistic capabilities to achieve altruistic goals. Also, to help others, there is a sense of self-satisfaction that some may define it as selfishness.

I grant that pure egoism is possible, but pure altruism is impossible – altruism must coexist with a bit of selfishness. When we appear to act unselfishly, other reasons might be hidden behind it, like a returned favor, the boost our reputation, or simply to feel good about oneself.

There are many parallels between Oedipus' story and Gorman's time on earth. Gorman, had to establish himself first to gain fame and wealth before he became charitable.

As far as I am concern, there is no debate here – Gorman was both.

Oedipus on the other hand, his acts were self-centered, to make himself look good, although people saw him as the man who could save them from horrible things to come. I have to admit that I feel some pity for him because his life was tormented by the gods. But, his egoism surfaced repeatedly, especially when he was more concerned that his image would be damaged by the accusation that he murdered King Laius. He seemed appalled at the thought that he may have done something wrong.

Becoming familiar with the play again, I found it interesting when he was speaking to Creon, accusing others of his shortcoming – a scene so familiar to some of today's world leaders.

Oedipus also wanted to keep his throne and save himself, even though he was a bad ruler - sound familiar?

Oedipus wrote his destiny. He did not examine his actions from the perspective of the prophecy but instead from what he wanted his fate to be; the ruler of a city who wanted to be remembered as a savior, the one who saves the city from the plague – it was too little too late.

To summarize, the king gained his reputation by his ruling decisions while Gorman almost tainted his in the last few years of his life, being self-inflicted with concerns of mortality.

He too, even so temporarily, abandoned the prophecies of his ancestors but fortunately for Gorman he left behind works of beauty and a gentle spirit, unlike Oedipus who left behind destruction.

R.C. Gorman died of a bacterial infection at the age of seventy-four on November 3, 2005.

As expected there were endless crowds in his funeral. The only place to accommodate the immense crowds coming to say their last goodbuys to the town's favorite son was the Sagebrush Inn Convention Center; it was full of people with more standing outside.

Flags flew at half-staff in his honor. Representatives of many different tribes of Native Americans attended the ceremony. There were dignitaries, celebrities, people from all walks of life, wearing T-shirts, jeans, boots, moccasins, business suits, bolo ties, and yes, Hawaiian shirts and bandannas. Governor Richardson and his wife Barbara attended. She spoke about their friendship with R.C. about his generosity and called him witty and brilliant. He was buried in a simple handmade cedar casket lined with his trademark headbands.

He was wrapped in a colorful Navajo blanket.

While the world will remember him for his beautiful art, those who live in Taos will remember him for so much more.

One of his friends told me, years after R.C.'s passing, that it seemed surreal for her watching R.C. laying in his casket. "I was expecting him to stand up, open his arms, laugh and say – Welcome, welcome friends. Thank you for coming."

That is how she wants to remember him.

Nocturne

Chinle Ruby

Maripossa II

27

THE ESTATE

Since the art market inflates after death, the importance of securing the artist's estate becomes a paramount concern for beneficiaries. Along with the general increase in cost for art pieces, the probate process becomes more frustrating, usually because of greed and rivalry often resulting in irreparable wounded feelings.

Consequently, it is common for the conflicting parties to end up worse overall financially since the only ones guaranteed to benefit from a sizable estate are the lawyers.

The ugly side of art's high prices is the intense fighting between inheritors and trustees. For instance, in Picasso's estate a settlement took six years and over thirty million to negotiate. With Dalí's estate, decades after his death, certain works of his are still debated.

Some artists who devoted their lifetime doing what they loved most, expressed the desire that their art should be displayed publicly beyond their death.

During the infighting for R.C. Gorman's estate, his legacy was in jeopardy while his artwork was collecting dust, waiting to sort out the probate mess. This was against his wishes.

Other artists, like Rothko's written wish, was that his art not to be locked up in a rooms of the very wealthy but be displayed for all to enjoy.

Andy Warhol, brilliantly stated that an artist's death means a lot of money to others and that he rather see the money go to his estate and charity than lawyers. Pollock and Lichtenstein among others followed that logic. Thomas Kinkade, Francis Bacon, Rivera, are some of the artists who after their death, the disputes over their estates, turned to dramatic courtroom showdowns. There are some cases where the recipients came to their senses and settled out of court, averting a real-life drama. Like in the case of Kinkade's estate where the dispute between his girlfriend and his wife, who after a bitter feud, decided to settle out of court. I have always found the subject of death and wealth intriguing.

In my humble opinion, the devastating loss and the material gain should be two potentially contradictory poles of logic.

It is difficult for me to comprehend what oratorical or psychological shrewdness persuades people to destroy relationships with loved ones over wealth.

In Gorman's case, the conflicts began once it was announced that he had a short time to live. Things didn't get any easier after his passing. R.C. Gorman's wishes were clear. He trusted Virginia to handle his estate and keep his legacy intact. He was also clear that the bulk of his estate shall go to his siblings, Virginia, and his various charities. But, it took more than six years of resentful feuding in probate court, before the estate was settled.

Some of the disputes were about his liquor collection, potted plants, rugs, sterling silver, lamps, and sculptures. On the serious side, one of the lawsuits was by a former art assistant and trusted Gorman's friend. He claimed he had painted some of Gorman's later work and was asking for fifteen million dollars.

It is not unusual for assistants to claim ownership of paintings after the passing of the real artist. Georgia O'Keeffe's and Andy Warhol's estates, among others, had to deal with similar claims.

Virginia who most likely spent every waking moment with R.C. disputed the claim. She asked to give the assistant a piece of paper and see what he could draw. "He could never do the Gorman images." she stated.

I believe that there are only a few things in life that unmask our strength, beauty, and ugliness like when it comes to gaining wealth and fame over others.

A few years into the probate mess, Gorman's lawyers approved the sale of his mansion to pay off the estate tax obligations. The house in Las Colonials was sold to a private school for two and a half million, with one million upfront. Half of that went to pay back property taxes. But, after the buyers failed to make payments, the property went to auction and Gorman's estate repurchased it for half a million dollars.

The once beautiful house was left ravaged and most items destroyed or stolen.

About a year after his death things got more complicated when his most trusted person, Virginia Dooley, went into a two-week coma that left her incapacitated, Gorman's attorneys were brought in to replace her. In the end, the only money winners were the attorneys, who kept piling up the hours and eventually were accused of milking the case for legal fees. The district court judge who was overseeing the case ordered their replacement with a court-appointed attorney.

By now lawsuits and claims were going every which way, a real mess to be untangled.

Eventually, no evidence found in the fifteen million claim of the former assistant and the state district judge dismissed the claim against the estate of R.C. Gorman.

A half a dozen potential buyers were bidding for the estate. Most of them were wealthy people from various states who simply wanted to buy the property and art. One of them, Bob Sahd was the only one with a plan on how to keep Gorman's legacy alive.

Admittedly at first Mr. Sahd's interest was about its potential investment value. However, in a time when the economy had devastated real estate markets, he was taking a risk that his investment would pay off. Bob Sahd is a successful real estate developer with projects in several southwestern states. Knew that being involved with the art business was a risky new venture for him, but he had confidence in his business ability. Additionally, he grew up in Taos and was aware of Gorman's vast following.

He was counting on Gorman's reputation to make the deal pay off.

When the entire estate was sold to Bob Sahd, half of the final sale price went to attorneys for legal fees. Once taxes were paid, Gorman's four siblings, Virginia's estate and the R.C. Gorman Foundation each received much less of what was left of the once substantial R.C. Gorman's estate.

The days that an artist's estate was a collection of art to be sold at an auction house are long gone. After so many cases where the estate recipients received much less than they should have through an auction, they wised up and found creative ways to make the most of their art. Now, most estate disputes involve art dealers dealing directly with galleries to handle the art left behind.

Usually, artists' estates are cash poor and art rich, therefore there is a strong motivation to bring the artist's work to a greater renown and a possible larger payoff when sold in a gallery.

Bob Sahd understood this situation well. So, when he bought R.C. Gorman's estate, he opened his galleries to sell the art directly to the public.

Since I found the fight over estates the ultimate pettiness I wanted to devote as little time as possible in this subject, simply because it is not important to R.C. Gorman's legacy. However, I want to emphasize Mr. Sahd's critical role in reviving the R.C. Gorman legacy.

Since Bob Sahd, gained possession of R.C. Gorman's estate, Gorman's associates and some employees were in fierce opposition to the way he wanted to handle Gorman's art. The opposition was about the reproduction of Gorman's art and the concern was that, under the new ownership, the charm of the Navajo gallery would no longer exist.

Let me think for a moment. The estate included a destroyed home on Las Colonias and a run-down studio on Ledoux Street, with dusty wooden cabinets full of Gorman's art inventory of unsold artwork. It doesn't seem that whoever was handling the business before was doing that well.

I am not certain how much charm was left but, what I am certain is that after Gorman's death there was a short resurgence of business, but after the infighting, there was pretty much nothingness. Not to mention the plundering of his home and the looting of his art; it was an insult to

R.C. Gorman's legacy.

Things got worse after Virginia's death.

Bob Sahd wrote a large check to buy the estate. Therefore, it was his business to do whatever he thought would be beneficial for his investment. He remodeled the Ledoux Street gallery and made staffing changes to reopened with a fresh start, and he did a massive renovation to the crumbling structure of Gorman's house in Las Colonias.

Since 2011, when Bob Sahd took over Gorman's estate, whatever steps he has taken to bring back Gorman's popularity and respect is working. Besides the initial investment to buy the estate and renovate the properties, Mr. Sahd invested in opening six R.C. Gorman Navajo Galleries throughout the southwest.

He has revived R.C. Gorman's popularity single-handedly. And, he is not done yet. He is planning to open more galleries in different cities to keep Gorman's legacy alive.

"At first it was all about business for me," he told me in an interview, "but, being around his work and seeing people's reaction to it, I grew to love his art even more. I am on a mission to make sure the everyone knows about Gorman's art."

Consequently, after Bob Sahd took over the R.C. Gorman estate, Gorman's work has been revived and the art production has elevated to an immense increased output.

Like the Phoenix in Greek mythology which is a symbol of renewal and rebirth. It is the majestic red and gold feathered bird that died in flames and obtains a new life by arising from the ashes. This stunning creature was associated with the pure sunlight, hence the nickname of Firebird, which, according to Herodotus, has a lifespan of over five hundred years before its life cycle repeats; from ashes to rise.

28

INSEPARABLE

Rose Roybal and Virginia Dooley, along with R.C. Gorman assembled an impressive team during R.C.'s rise to prominence. Rose was more than Gorman's housekeeper and cook. She and R.C. went to the farmer's market often, especially in the later years, and after having fun shopping, they went home and cooked together. Rose and Virginia traveled with R.C. alternating between destinations. Virginia went to the cities with historic museums, notable theaters, and music halls. R.C. took Rose along to the cities with the best restaurants and to Spanish speaking countries to translate the language.

At home, Rose was the protagonist during their famous dinner parties with celebrities. She was Gorman's pillar of strength in doubtful moments and the motherly figure that kept him grounded. Theirs was a friendship that bonded strongly through difficult times and it was tender in good times.

Virginia Dooley was the center of Gorman's universe. She was his protector and his promoter. No one could get close to Gorman without a first passing inspection by her. In their spare time, they loved to play piano and sing songs together.

Gorman's refined treatment towards these two women, revealed his gentle spirit.

When Rose died in 2002, the bond of the three broke.

Gorman sank into a deep depression. Life somehow did not seem the same and the void Rose left behind appeared irreplaceable. While in public he wore happy faces, smiling on the outside while slowly dying on the inside. His already failing health began to deteriorate.

It is true that behind every great man there is a great woman. R.C. Gorman was fortunate to have two great women in his life who cared deeply for him.

It is known that Gorman had an avoidance reaction towards death. In fact, when someone that he knew died, he became depressed. I know the feeling well. Growing up in a small community, during funerals processions, I've seen so much hurting on friendly faces that my empathy for the loss of life sunk deeply into my young psyche. Now I try to avoid funerals at any cost.

I grew up in a culture of dramatic reactions to every celebration and ceremony. I became familiar with the drama of death and broken hearts of those left behind.

The concept of a broken heart renewed notoriety recently, after Carrie Fisher's death, when her mother died unexpectedly a day later.

When loved ones die in quick succession; the second death is often contributed to a broken heart. According to science, the broken heart syndrome is a real thing.

The Greeks created drama for a reason. Since the ancient times, the ceremonies were a measured hysteria. During the Greek dramatic performances in the theater, there was a chaos of lamenting, passion, and excessive emotions.

The question is, is the entire emotional uproar necessary to mend the emotional wounds?

Historians attribute the hysteric rampages, especially by women during funerals, to be a healing process - to transgress social boundaries and get it out of your system.

Consequently, the way people grieve and bury their dead in my culture has not changed much since classical times, except perhaps in the big cities. There is still a large amount of drama. I've witnessed people distraught, collapsing in cemeteries and even willing to throw themselves into the grave to be buried with their loved one.

After seeing the grief-stricken reaction of mourners, I am convinced that a broken heart is real – I've seen people, strong people defeated by dominant pain.

When Gorman himself passed away, Virginia's heart was broken.

It was she who launched an aggressive early publicity campaign to introduce R.C. Gorman's work to a wider audience. For more than three decades, Virginia kept up the combative promotion that helped Gorman establish his artistic legacy.

Virginia Dooley said once - I live to watch him draw. She obviously meant it. Her life lost its meaning without her R.C.

A year after Gorman's death and failing health, Virginia went into a coma that left her incapacitated until she died two years later.

During their time together the love between these three individuals ascended into an unbroken spiritual bonding, reflecting the concept of *Platonic Love.*

Although the *Republic*, provides Plato's philosophy, blending politics, ethics, metaphysics, moral psychology, and epistemology, it is his writings in the *Symposium,* dated around 375 BC, that reflects his theory of *Twin Souls* and *Platonic Love.*

In the *Symposium,* during his dialogue with Socrates, Plato has to think deeply, as Socrates uses his famous *Socratic Method* of questioning, to enforce Plato to articulate his ideas and answers.

It is then when he writes about *The Ladder of Love,* a guide on how to ascend to the beauty of love. This dialogue leads their narrative to Plato's introduction of the *Twin Flames* and the merging of the twin-souls.

During the same dialogue, Plato writes about how the feeling of love evolves, both sexually and non-sexually. In his non-sexual theory, the *Platonic Love,* begins from a beautiful attraction but transcends gradually to love for the supreme beauty of mind and soul.

Maybe it is time for someone to come up with the concept of Triplet Souls, to reflect the relationship between, R.C., Virginia and Rose.

29

THE CATALYST

As the airplane descended into the Phoenix airport, I watched the endless blue sky of Arizona become a canvas of spectacular colors. After its long trek over the greenery of the desert, the sun was about to set. There are two spectacular sunsets that enslave my senses. This one over the Arizona desert and its rugged mountains and the one in Santorini over the turquoise-blue waters of my beautiful homeland.

In both places when the sun touches the surface of the mountains or the sea, the sky erupts with brilliant colors of yellow, gold and red. Brilliant, just like Gorman's paintings.

As I stepped outside the airport, a few clouds appeared in the southern sky while a gentle breeze blew, bringing some relief to the desert heat.

I had one more stop to make before getting home. Something was stewing in my brains and when this happens, I can not relax. Mysteries are my Achilles heel.

I was perplexed with the ongoing criticism about the person who bought Gorman's estate, even though he was responsible for R.C. Gorman's renewed immense popularity.

Located on the original town-site of Scottsdale, is the historic district known as Old Town Scottsdale. The ambiance is old world Scottsdale; a blend of southwestern flair, contemporary arts, great restaurants, unique shops, and active nightlife. This historic territory is one of Arizona's most charming places.

In the heart of Old Town, is the Scottsdale Art District, featuring hundreds of art galleries, displaying the works of art by thousands of artists. The centerpiece of the Art District is Main Street.

As I walked on Main Street towards R.C. Gorman's Navajo art gallery, numerous art lovers began to build momentum for the customary Thursday night art walk.

Bob Sahd was waiting for me inside the gallery. I had asked him if he had time to take a walk and talk about his decision to get involved with R.C. Gorman's estate. Outside, in the aftermath of a gentle rain, there was an earthborn refreshing breath of freshness.

"The attorney handling the probate, Mr. Millet, was calling prospective buyers for Gorman's estate. Because of my business ties to Taos, I was one of the people he contacted. I believe Mr. Millet was determined to find a buyer because the probate was dragging on for too long." Bob said as we were strolling through the Art District.

What was your reaction at first?

"I was interested. I grew up in Taos and knew about Gorman's popularity." Were there others who were interested in the estate?

"There were seven others." He went on to explain that he became increasingly excited at the thought of buying Gorman's Estate, even though he knew very little about the art business. But, once he decided to make his move, there was no hesitation.

"Remember, this was a time of high-interest rates and no financial availability from the banks. Even so, I wanted to get involved." he added. What do you think turned the tide your way?

"I believe the fact that I was a local businessman and a real estate developer played a major role. But what closed the deal was when I went to see Gorman's siblings, his two sisters and his brother, and asked them what was important to them. All three of them wanted Gorman's legacy to live on. I promised them that it would be my priority. I believe that I kept my promise."

What was your reaction when you learned that you were chosen?

"First let me say that it was a business decision. It was a business opportunity for sure. But the moment I heard that I was chosen, I got really excited."

Okay. You bought the estate. Now what?

"Now I had to come up with the money. Since the banks were not giving loans, I had to borrow some money from friends."

Well, what about after the estate was sold to you?

"To tell you the truth, I did not even know what was there. I mean, I knew the properties and the art displayed in the gallery and in his home but, I was pleasantly surprised to find hundreds of pieces of art in the upstairs cabinets of the gallery on Ledoux Street. That was the moment that I seriously thought about the reproduction of Gorman's art."

I know there were some very disgruntled employees when you took over. They resisted the changes. What did you think about that?

"Look. I think big. This is my nature. The small gallery on Ledoux Street was romantic and all, but I wanted a bigger gallery. I wanted to open R.C. Gorman's Navajo Galleries in many cities."

I think, people did not realize that, besides the investment of buying the estate, there was so much more investment needed; to build galleries, hire more employees. Was this a concern?

"Yes. But before I started thinking about expanding the art gallery business, I had to remodel Gorman's house in order to sell it. A year after I bought the estate which included the art gallery in Taos. I then opened galleries in Santa Fe and Albuquerque. Later on I opened art galleries in Scottsdale, and then Sedona and Tubac."

Why Arizona?

"When I decided to go to Arizona, some people questioned that decision. They suggested that cities with busier art markets would be better. But, I wanted to open new frontiers. I felt Arizona was the perfect place to start, especially because it is where art lovers go to find Native American Art. R.C. Gorman is revered in New Mexico but he is popular in Arizona as well."

What is next for Bob Sahd?

"I want to open more Gorman galleries, in every city and around the world. My next target is Los Angeles and Las Vegas."

I shook my head and said - But you are so busy right now. I know it is hard to keep up with you. You are here today, in Santa Fe tomorrow, running from city to city. Why are you doing this to yourself?

"As I said earlier, when I got involve with Gorman's estate it was about business. It is no longer the case. I have fallen in love with Gorman's work. Day after day, I see the reaction of the people about his art and makes me feel good that his work brings happiness to so many people. The main reason that keeps me going it is not just business – it is a labor of love."

Bob Sahd does not talk much about his personal art collections. However, it is widely claimed that he has one of the largest art collection owned by one person.

We walked between the crowds going in and out the galleries. I was happy to see so many people interested in the arts.

Night had fallen. The bright lights illuminated Main Street. Some entertainers were performing on the sidewalks. I saw an old friend, Dante, who used to perform in the Author's Cafe, our family coffee shop we opened in the Art District a few years back to promote young upcoming artists, writers, poets, actors and musicians.

Dante was a bit older now but still doing what he loves to do most; play his music. "Take care of this man" he shouted at Bob pointing at me and smiling, then respectfully bowed his head. As we walked back into his gallery, Bob rushed to talk to his customers. He seemed happy in his element and his love for the Gorman's art seemed genuine.

This is what R.C. wanted, someone to carry on his legacy. "Look," he said just before rushing in the gallery, "My family was fortunate because of the generosity of a gentleman who was a good friend of my Dad. He had no other family and we welcomed him into our family. When he became terminally ill, he decided to leave the La Fonda Hotel in Taos, to my Dad. It was because of his generosity that my family started in business. I will never forget that gesture and I always try to help people." By now I knew Bob Sahd well and there was no reason to doubt his sincerity. He looked at me; his face brightened with a wide smile, he tapped on my shoulder and said. "The friend who left us the hotel was a Greek man. I have a great affinity for Greek people."

That was good enough for me - to like this man a bit more.

My big Greek family has now accepted Bob as one of our own.

I stood by the door of the Navajo Gallery for a few moments. I was remembering a couple of years ago, walking in the gallery with so little knowledge about Gorman – it has been a great journey.

After seeing what Bob Sahd is doing, I thought that he should be the hero to millions of Gorman's fans around the world for keeping the beloved artist's legacy alive.

Art lovers were walking in the gallery empty handed, while others were walking out with a piece of Gorman's art to take home.

If R.C. were here, he would be walking by the door, smiling, waving, and saying in good humor - Thank you for your money!

No. Mr. Gorman. Thank you for your art.

30

PROUD LADY

Twenty-four years before his passing, when R.C. Gorman was crossing the bridge to prominence, he began his serious quest not only to evaluate the definition of his art but also a quest for inclusive self-examination as well.

I mentioned earlier that I believe Gorman carefully cultivated his bigger-than-life persona. Gorman understood that the fundamental concern for artists who want to earn wide recognition and respect is that the essence of their work reflects a powerful message.

Hidden behind Gorman's gregarious personality were traces of sadness.

It was after his experience with the spirited art of Mexico that he began to clarify the ugliness of life by creating images of beauty – just like the muralists had done.

R.C. Gorman was not concerned with the status quo but rather with reality to spark our imagination, to fill the emptiness of the beauty within.

Gorman's art was sometimes imperfect, sometimes beautiful but always raw and real.

The earlier underlying sadness in his art slowly disappeared throughout the years. At first, there was the silent pain of the loss of young lives, his friend in San Francisco and his brother Kee; sadness that stubbornly perched at the edge of his consciousness.

Then there was natural anger aimed towards his father leaving him during most of his childhood years. An emotion that began to heal when he realized that his Dad was missing because of a noble reason - to serve his country. His anger subsided during his Dad's near-death ordeal.

On the contrary, the issues about his mother leaving his father for another man while serving his country remained unsolved for years to come.

Seven years after his mother's death and twenty-four years before leaving his earthly life behind, R.C. Gorman drew a sketch he called *Proud Mother*.

I believe that it was of a great importance to him for his mother to be proud of him.

As the years went by R.C. Gorman worked hard to produce his art and to handle his business wisely. He published books. He received great honors, he did exhibitions in prestigious institutes and received several honorary doctorate degrees. During all of these, the image of the little boy from Chinle with a stick for a brush and red mud for paint remained vividly within him. The horse rides through the heart of America's amazing and unforgettable land, the panoramic views of jagged rocks, sandstone pinnacles, and flat orange mesas. The sacred mountains surrounded by sagebrush and pinon pines, with wild mustangs and burros roaming around, and sheep grazing on their slopes, remained intact in his mind.

However, the sketch of *Proud Mother* remained unfinished.

During the frantic dash to artistic immortality, Gorman neglected to deal with his mother's issue. After his mother's death, the fumes of anger eventually faded away and became intolerable guilt for not expressing his love to her.

It was a sentiment that haunted him for a long time.

The sketch of *Proud Mother* was now hidden in the darkness of a drawer.

"I will walk to the highest mountain to light a candle for my mother." Gorman stated later in life.

Every time I visited one of his Galleries, I kept looking at the image of *Proud Lady*. I was perplexed about its attractiveness to so many people.

I wasn't sure why I liked it.

During my many interactions with Gorman's admirers, I could understand why a certain piece emotionally moved people. Like the elder gentleman from Oregon, choked up with emotions while looking at the images of the *Enigma Suite*. "Are you okay my friend?" I asked. "I just need a moment," he said. Then he turned to me and continued, "I did not know much about Gorman's art." his voice trembled. He took a deep breath and continued "My wife just passed away. These pieces are so intense. I could not help thinking of her."

It is this strange melancholy we feel when we face true beauty in a piece of profound art. It is that longing, that we can't quite describe when we witness something truly meaningful.

"I keep a box of Kleenex in my desk" One of the sales clerks of the Santa Fe Gorman's gallery, told me once.

I remembered the lady who was transfixed with *Mariposa*, the butterfly sitting on the woman's shoulder, looking at each other, as if they were carrying a conversation. Her joy was overwhelming.

"What is so special about this one?" I asked.

"This is my mother's favorite. I am shipping it to Seattle for her," Her face illuminated with a smile, thinking of her mother's joy when she receives her gift. "Let me show you my favorite." She walked towards the *Proud Lady*. "This is it," she said.

This one again! I still don't get it.

She continued talking, "I look at it before I go to bed and it is the first thing I see when I wake up." She raised her shoulders slightly and painted a confounded expression on her face. "I am not sure what it is about this but I cannot be without it," she said.

She walked away while I stood for a while looking at the *Proud Lady*. The image of the white-dressed woman was enclosed in the iconic Gorman's curved lines, her crossed legs resembled the shape of a heart. Her facial expression was overcome with pride and power.

On my way home, I was still puzzled about the effect the *Proud Lady* had on people. As I said mysteries are my nemesis.

Nobody could convince me that during his frantic dash to create an enormous amount of art in the eighties and the nineties he did not have the time to complete the *Proud Lady*. It seems that this one was the elephant in Gorman's studio.

By now he realized that it was his mother who took care of him. However, he idolized his father who just dropped by from time to time to see them.

What is wrong with this picture?

It was his mother that directed him towards a new world and encouraged him to learn about new cultures beyond the reservation. It was she who took him out of the Navajo reservation and enrolled him in Ganado Mission School, a place that encouraged him to follow his heart as an artist. Granted, his father did the same and he was instrumental in helping R.C.'s growth as an artist and helped him immensely to promote his art. They both deserved R.C.'s respect.

Sitting by his window, overlooking his mountains, he reflected on the past.

The evolution of his artistic creativity grew in stages; the earth and the desert landscape of rocks and canyons rubbed off and became people, beautiful images and bright colors.

The evolution of his artistic soul and his ongoing quest to capture a person's spirit in his drawings allowed him to grow personally along with his art. He evolved as a person who wanted to help others and to leave behind the charm of expressionism.

His personal struggles mean nothing to me; it is part of our growth as humans to find our identity - in retrospect, his struggles helped him rather than hindered him.

The evidence is in his very latest works; seeing how far away his later work had gone from his original ones is an understanding of his vision. It shows his ability to evolve as an artist.

From the humble drawings taken to the trading post, his art evolved into captivated images. Yes, he partied hard and drank and wore better clothes and ate better foods – so what? That should not be a part of his artistic legacy.

The poor kid in the reservation, walking with shoes full of holes and ragged clothes and grew up to be R.C. Gorman – This is the importance of the story here. The rest is gossip for ephemeral news.

There are many artists that possess this strange ability to create magic every time they held a pencil or a brush and started drawing on a blank surface.

R.C. Gorman was one of them.

"Youth is what important. Live it to the fullest. When you grow old, you sit back and reflect." He said once.

I believed he was satisfied with his legacy while sitting by his window reflecting. And, yes, he was saddened leaving the "good life" behind but nothing new here; the fear of death is a natural reaction.

I want to believe that Gorman knew that his selfishness were the major obstacle to forgive himself for disappointing his mother.

It was then that the *Proud Mother* became the *Proud Lady* - The last piece he finalized before his death.

I get it now. The *Proud Lady* personifies Gorman's incredible journey, his joyfulness, his sadness, the celebrations, and the loneliness. All his emotions are entangled in this seemingly simple image and trapped within his amazing curving lines.

When people ask me why the *Proud Lady* is my very favorite Gorman painting, it is difficult to explain my feelings in a fleeting conversation. I cannot define that image in a sentence, all I could do is to shrug my shoulders and simply tell them, "Please, read my book."

Whatever you might think of Gorman, the fact remains that before moving to Taos the art community there had lost its charm. R.C. Gorman was Taos' greatest ambassador. I would argue that his passing has been a critical factor in the continued steep decline of the Taos art market.

The last time I left Taos, I visited R.C. Gorman's graveside. He lies at rest by his home in Las Colonias, under his beloved mountains, surrounded by wild flowers and facing the sun.

"Rest in peace, my friend."

It was time for me to rest as well, knowing full well that R.C. Gorman's legacy lives on.

My long journey of Gorman's life was on an enduring curving road. The life on it, sometimes beautiful, sometimes broken but nevertheless redeeming.

Proud Mother

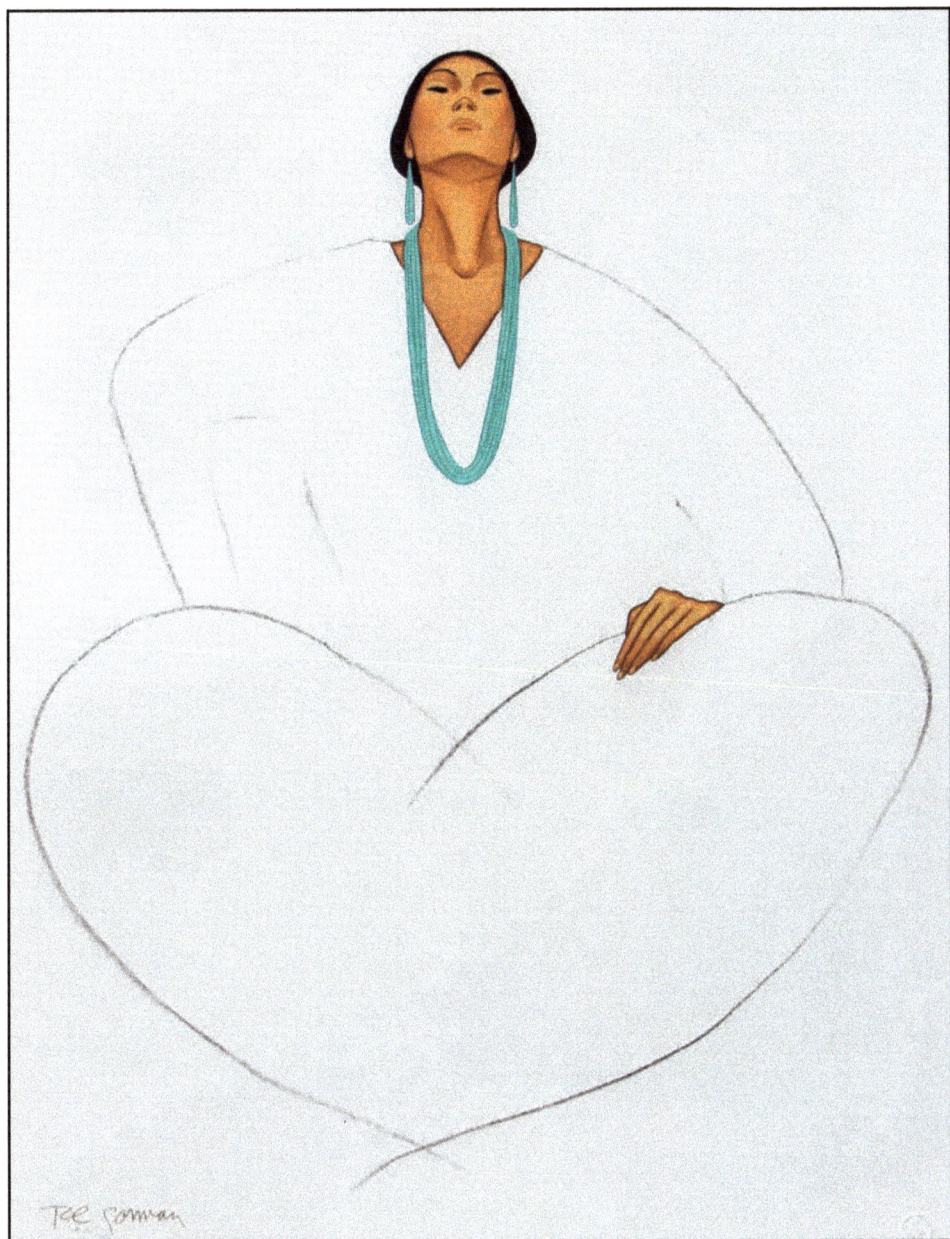

Proud Lady

Nikos Ligidakis

About the Author

Award winning author, Nikos Ligidakis, writes with clarity and passion in an ardent voice, not to just recount adventures, but with an expression of feelings, to encourage the reader to think, to find hope in the eternal struggle for the meaning of life and the awareness of harmony.

In his award winning book, *The Last Mission*, Ligidakis introduces a hero in a fascinated story of survival during World War II. This incredible story narrates this hero's freedom run of hundreds of miles in an enemy territory full of danger, exhaustion, starvation, and death.

His culinary books, *5024 E. McDowell, A Man's Journey Into Culinary Exploration and My Private Collection of Pieces of Art, Dessert Recipes Of A Master*, Ligidakis demonstrates his priceless culinary knowledge, gained during his days as a celebrated chef.

Power and Defiance, The Human Struggle for Social Justice, it is the book Ligidakis calls, "The work of my lifetime." It is a labor of love, a nearly eight hundred page saga about the integrity of individual freedom and the intense struggle for social justice. Such deep matter requires not only the profound thoughts in writing but also the equal reflective thoughts in the reading.

His latest book, *The Extraordinary Life of Bill O'Brien, An Ordinary Arizona Irish Cowboy*, is an inspirational story of adventure, excitement, achievement, the importance of character and how an "ordinary Arizona Irish Cowboy" overcame obstacles and challenges to achieve success in unique and creative ways. An entertaining and compelling narrative about one of Arizona's most fascinated characters.

The Power of His Brush, The Evolution of R.C. Gorman, is Ligidakis' ninth book.

www.ingramcontent.com/pod-product-compliance
Lightning Source LLC
Chambersburg PA
CBHW040407110426
42812CB00011B/2481